The Joy of Compassionate Connecting

The Way of Christ through Nonviolent Communication

*How blest are those who know their need for God,
for the Kingdom of Heaven is theirs.* (Matthew 5:3, NEB)

*Then Jesus said, "Come to me, all of you who are weary and carry
heavy burdens, and I will give you rest. Take my yoke upon you. Let
me teach you, because I am humble and gentle at heart, and you will
find rest for your souls. For my yoke is easy to bear, and the burden I
give you is light."* (Matthew 11:28–30, NLT)

If you follow my teachings, you are really my disciples. (John 8:31, NIV)

*This is how everyone will recognize that you are my disciples — when
they see the love you have for each other.* (John 13:35, *The Message*)

The Joy of Compassionate Connecting

The Way of Christ through Nonviolent Communication

Jaime L. Prieto, Jr.

Compassionate Connecting
Aliso Viejo, California
www.CompassionateConnecting.com

(That's the legalese. Please consider supporting my efforts to contribute to the well-being of others by buying a copy of the book. If you can't afford the paperback, let me know and I'll try to get you one, thereby, supporting my mission).

Holy Bible, New International Version. Copyright 1973, 1978, 1984 by International Bible Society. Used by permission of Zondervan.

Holy Bible, New Living Translation, copyright 1996, 2004, 2007. Used by permission of Tyndale House Publishers, Inc.

Holy Bible, New English Bible, Copyright 1961, 1970. Used by permission of Oxford University Press, and Cambridge University Press.

The Message: The Bible In Contemporary Language, Copyright 1993, 1994, 1995, 1996, 2000, 2001, 2002. Used by permission of NavPress Publishing Group.

ISBN 978-0-557-66432-0 (hardcover)

ISBN 978-1-451-51425-4 (paperback)

Library of Congress Control Number: 2010913657

Cover design by Lori Yost.

This book is provided for information and educational purposes only. It does not contain or constitute psychological or health advice, which must be addressed by a licensed therapist or physician.

About the front cover: I remember my Dad telling me about two ceiba trees at the entrance of his hometown in Quebradillas, Puerto Rico. He said the trees were around when Christopher Columbus discovered America. I imagine the Tree of Life looking like that in the Garden of Eden. This photo is a perfect visual introduction for this book.

The ceiba tree equals life. The wall equals judgment, which prevents us from connecting with each other. The highway running past the ceiba tree equals the strategies we choose that are not serving the gift of life. We run right past the Tree of Life and toward a fleeting illusion of joy down the road when we pass by the choice that brings lasting joy.

About the back cover: A photo taken from my hotel room in Oahu, Hawaii, of two doves perched in my balcony. Doves are symbols of peace and also of the Holy Spirit. I enjoyed their symmetry. One was looking inside into my room, and the other was looking outside. I also enjoy the contrast of light in the background. I see this photo as a metaphor for two aspects of Christ needed for connection: grace and truth.

Contents

Poetry

Art

Photos

Figures

Acknowledgments

I am deeply grateful to the people who reviewed the early manuscript and helped me see how the story is unfolding: Robert Thompson, Garret Weeks, Julie Shiposh, Sheri Denham, David Bryan Esch, Mary Mackenzie, Leonard Szymczak, Terry LePage, Sherri Boles-Rogers, Barbara Deckmeyer (editor, friend), and the editing team at Lulu.com.

I thank these people who gave me feedback, support, and encouragement: Cecilia Prieto Morehouse, Lori Yost, Tamara LaPorte, D'Marie Mulatierri, Sister Karen Sammons, Philip McKeon, Kundan Chabra, Jim Manske, Father Christlin Rajendram, Adrian Godina, Yvette Erasmus, Craig Preston, Jeanine Noguera, Lars, Shaunna Bach, Roberta Wall, Dan Tocchini and Loreene Weeks. Special thanks to my Composition II teacher, Walter Klarner, who contributed to shifting my attitude toward writing so writing became enjoyable.

I am grateful to Dr. Marshall Rosenberg, the founder of NVC, whose Center for Nonviolent Communication can be visited at www.cnvc.org. I also want to acknowledge Upgeya Pew (who introduced me to NVC and facilitated my first practice group in 2002), and Ellen Shiro for facilitating practice groups when I really needed them. These friends helped me understand NVC in my early days. I thank the NVC community, who live in harmony with their values, for supporting my needs for authenticity, integrity, and connection.

I am grateful to my *ekklesia* community of Christ followers who helped me grow spiritually and encouraged me on my path. As we gather in our homes, go for hikes and trips, play, celebrate, and mourn, they enable me to experience a new kind of church geared toward meeting the needs of its people as we embrace and celebrate Christ in our midst. To Garret Weeks, The Shiposhes (Bryan, Julie, Sage, Sierra), Vivian Soo, Nathan Kolta, and all those who make up the people I consider my community: The Estado 29 orphanage kids and supporters, my "Christ Renews His Parish" (CHRP) family, the men who "Stand In the Gap," "mi familia Boricua," my "De La Salle" brotherhood, Gary and Steve's "Micah 6:8" Bible study group at Mariners, Friday CDM beach volleyballers, my Camp Recovery friends, La Vida Drum Circle in Aliso Beach, Doheny Beach surfers, Rock Harbor Wild At Heart men's group, Thursday Night Men's Group, Compassionate Leadership 2010, Michael's "Soul Motion" dance community, and all the poets, artists, musicians, hikers, rock climbers, skiers and snowboarders I have met along the way.

I also thank my dad, whose example of service inspires me to contribute. He taught me about autonomy. His message of wisdom is to respect others, no matter their religion, political leanings, cultural background, socioeconomic status, or gender.

I am deeply grateful to my mother, Cece, who lives in the Garden and is part of it. She taught me about spirituality at an early age, and she gave me love, encouragement, and understanding. I am deeply grateful for her contribution to my life, for the meals she prepared, for my education, for the flowers she planted, and for being a source of beauty for me.

To Alex Miguel, my son

Remember the scroll I gave you at John's Meadow?
This book is the next step.

I.

INTRODUCTION

This book is the result of my own journey into healthy and loving relationships by integrating the teachings of Jesus. I now see his words come to life in my own experience; how new language based on awareness of observations, feelings, needs, and requests (OFNR) has given me a new set of tools that support the foundation of loving relationships. I feel the deep peace and inner harmony of a life filled with meaning. I am now living life on purpose, filled with lots of joy. Some occasional sadness becomes joy as I give my heart a voice. This new language is called Nonviolent Communication, NVC for short.

After ten years or so of growing and participating in programs intended to improve relationships, I realized I still wanted a clearer path toward intimacy and connection. This book is intended to be spiritual but not religious. It is about connecting and, in so doing, healing parts of our hearts that long for love and intimacy every day. Our hearts contain all the vital information we need; as a matter of fact, we got everything we could ever need for a happy and fulfilling life straight from the source—God. As we open the hood and acknowledge our heart life, we begin to feel a natural curiosity and compassion toward others. From this place of inner peace, it becomes easier to connect with other people.

In my search for relationships that worked for me, I ran into NVC almost by accident. Four years or so after my divorce, I moved to South Orange County in California because I needed a change. I went to a friend's house, where a man named

Upgeya had just returned from a weeklong retreat and was bristling with excitement. He told us he was starting an eight-week practice group whose focus was on communicating clearly and with integrity. He said, "The process will help you find more connection and intimacy in your relationships. Would you like to join?"

That was in the spring of 2002. Today my life looks and feels a lot different from what it was back then. I feel much more joy and a deeper peace, as I am finally living in integrity with myself and others. My external self, the one I share with the world, is consistent with my inner self, the one I live with wherever I go. I have a clarity of mind that I did not think was possible, especially when it comes to responsibility. I now see where I am responsible and where I am not, freeing up a lot of emotional energy because I focus on what I have control over—me. I am more aware of my internal dialogue, of my own judgments, feelings, and needs. I also have the power to make clear requests of myself and others. All this leads me to experience joy through a new freedom and willingness to play as I let go of my judgments and accept myself and others as we are.

The self-awareness and the resulting joy that I feel inspire me to engage people in a dialogue of the heart. I am drawn to connect with other human beings, and I want to contribute to their well-being and to their freedom to live a full life.

The truth is, there's something in it for me. Once others are free and alive, I have more people to know and connect with, more people to play with in the sandbox called life. I have more people to share a meal with. I can join them to dance, sing, drum, or roll down a grassy hill.

This is also the message of Jesus: an invitation of love that invites us to see others as precious human beings and to fully accept ourselves as one of them. To live life on purpose, connected to the source of life that is God, and to remember the reason for which we came to be—to experience and share love!

I invite you to join me on this journey of healing our hearts and filtering out the chatter of our minds as we recognize how easy it is to get stuck there, disconnected from the heart. I invite you to hear how Jesus's words inspire us to live in loving relationships as we become aware of the elements of communicating compassionately.

Each chapter presented in this book is an invitation to follow the loving message of Jesus and to partake in the banquet of life as we find healing, forgiveness, peace, and love in our interactions with others and within ourselves. This invitation is to follow his teachings and to experience the grace and truth of Christ through the conversations we choose to have with ourselves and others. Building a clear awareness of the dynamics of conversation can open the door to a deeper experience of life through love. Jesus reminds us:

I have come that they may have life, and have it to the full.
(John 10:10b, NIV)

This book is divided into five sections, and is best understood if read from beginning to end. The first section is the introduction, where we are now. Here I offer an overview of NVC, a look at interpersonal and societal violence, and the good news that Jesus has for us.

The second section, "Echoes of the Garden," visits the book of Genesis and considers the birth of moral judgment as an effect of eating the fruit of the Tree of Knowledge of Good and Evil. We are also reminded of our creation and how God made us in his image and likeness, saying we are *very good*—inviting us to accept that we too are part of the Garden of Eden. This section explores how the creation story is still relevant today.

The third section, "Sermon of the Master," is focused on the message of Jesus from the canonical Gospels and how his message of love is used in communication: empathy is a form of grace, and honesty is a form of truth.

The fourth section, "Compassionate Connecting," focuses on the concepts and practice of NVC within a Christ-centered life.

In the final section, "Conversations in Closing," I wrap things up with some scripture to inspire the reader to ask, seek, and knock in search of the treasure.

1.

What Is NVC?

In *Nonviolent Communication: A Language of Life,* Marshall Rosenberg tells us that

> NVC is founded on language and communication skills that strengthen our ability to remain human even under trying conditions. It contains nothing new; all that has been integrated into NVC has been known for centuries. The intent is to remind us about what we already know—about how we humans were meant to relate to one another—and to assist us in living in a way that concretely manifests this knowledge. NVC guides us in reframing how we express ourselves and hear others. Instead of being habitual, automatic reactions, our words become conscious responses based firmly on an awareness of what we are perceiving, feeling, and wanting.[1]

The following is a summary of my understanding of NVC:

For me, NVC is a means to an end, not an end unto itself. It is a way of getting somewhere-not in a physical sense, but of transforming ourselves into a different being. NVC isn't necessarily the only way to get to this end, but it's one that seems to best facilitate the exchange of words that most closely describe where I find myself so that others can actually understand the intention behind what I expressed.

Through this usage and awareness of language, others will also be able to express themselves so that I have a chance of hearing and understanding the intention behind their words. Through this mutual hearing of our intentions, a deeper understanding that transcends the words emerges. This is how we open the door for the Holy Spirit and how we get a sense that we are not alone in the world—that we belong to something bigger than us and have something in common, perhaps something to share. This sharing is not necessarily of goods and services, but it can be of those too.

I'm guessing that for many people, the *end* can be different things. The word that seems to describe the end that NVC helps me to get to is *communion*—an intimate connection with the source of life from which we came and of which we share, God. Through this *common union*, we realize that we are intimately connected with each other in ways that we perhaps were not aware of before.

NVC helps me to develop the awareness that I need to become free of the things that get in the way of the intimate connection that I seek. It also provides a common way to use language that facilitates communicating with other human beings. It helps me to acknowledge the limitation of words yet to feel empowered and inspired to try to overcome that limitation. NVC helps me to have clear conversations so that I have the freedom and understanding to choose how I show up in life, to live authentically, with purpose and integrity.

One important goal of NVC is to improve the quality and depth of our communication with others, which is a requirement for fulfilling and loving relationships. We do this by becoming aware of our observations, feelings, needs, and requests of ourselves and others, or OFNR, and express them in our empathy and honesty. Learning NVC is like learning to play a musical instrument: once we have the basics down, we can start to create our own music instead of just listening and reacting to the music we hear. Be patient with yourself on this journey and realize that as you are learning NVC, you may also be unlearning old habits, which may take time.

Observation vs. Evaluation

The term *observation* invites us to separate what is actually happening from our evaluation of it. Think of describing what you see as a video camera sees it. Our evaluations are the extra things not recorded by the camera. Recognizing the distinction between observing and evaluating is vitally important in NVC. Our evaluations of a situation minimize our chances of connecting with ourselves and others; another word for evaluations is *judgments*. The phrase "don't judge your judgments" comes to mind as an invitation to acceptance.

Feelings

Feelings tell us whether our needs are being met. They are neither good nor bad, they just contain information about our experiences. Feelings are like the music of the heart. When our needs are met, we experience pleasant feelings such as joy, happiness, awe, and contentment—the music is harmonious. When needs are not met, we experience unpleasant feelings such as sadness, hurt, anxiety, fear, annoyance, and anger—the music is dissonant. Feelings are a door to wondrous connection and self-understanding, a key to our hearts. A reference list of feelings and needs appears at the end of this book.

Needs

Needs are aspects of life that we require and value, such as nutrition, safety, meaning, integrity, freedom, community, clarity, peace, celebration, beauty, and love. Needs are universal; everyone has them whether they are dormant or alive in us. They motivate our thoughts and actions. Our needs are like the instruments in an orchestra: not all instruments play at the same time; they take turns and sometimes play together. Recognizing our needs is a good first step toward getting them met with mutual satisfaction in a relationship and reaching an outcome of both sides being happy. An awareness of needs can minimize violence, facilitate conflict resolution, and help people find peace.

Requests

A request is a personal formulation of what would meet our needs and make life wonderful. Without the request, we remain in abstract thinking and are likely to experience an aimless wandering of disappointment and frustration. By formulating a request and verbalizing it to others on behalf of our hearts, we explore within and reveal to others what will make life wonderful for us, making it more likely that we'll experience pleasant feelings such as joy.

Empathy

We now apply our awareness of OFNR to being in empathy. In order to offer empathy to someone else, we must first identify and embrace our own feelings and needs through *self-empathy* to become present, or connected to, ourself. Empathy shared with another person is about being present with them, offering respectful listening and understanding of their experience, and acknowledging their feelings and needs, sometimes with words.

Honesty

Honesty is the counterpart to empathy. Honesty is expressing our inner experience to another person, without judgment, labeling, or criticism. They may have stimulated something in us but they are not the cause of that something. In NVC, honesty often takes the form of sharing our observation, feelings, and needs and making requests of the other person.

Self-Empathy

Empathy applied to ourselves is called *self-empathy* in NVC. Through the process of self-empathy, we strive to get clear with our current experience by inquiring about and identifying the feelings and needs that are stimulated in this moment. This connects us with our own heart, making connections with other people more likely.

Tying It All Together

The following diagram helps to put OFNR in the context of a conversation that we might have with ourselves as we acknowledge our heart and mind with self-empathy.

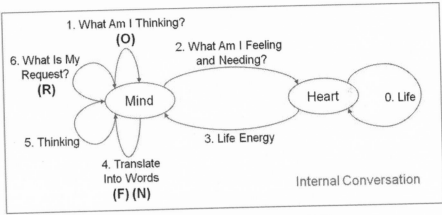

Figure 1. Self-Empathy State and OFNR

The state diagram above, which is a logical model of a dynamic system used in engineering, is a useful means of showing where we are focusing our attention.[2] When our attention is on mind things, we can visualize the Mind oval lighting up while the Heart oval remains dark. When we focus our attention on heart things, we can visualize the Heart oval as lighting up while the Mind oval remains dark.

The arrows represent activities we undertake; they have a starting point and an ending point. Sometimes an activity keeps us in the mind state; at other times we may move to the heart state.

The mind is the part of us that does all the thinking and analyzing. It is typically associated with the left hemisphere of the brain. The heart is the part of us that identifies closely with our bodies, our creativity, and life experience through feelings and needs, and it is typically associated with the brain's right hemisphere.[3]

Any time we feel something in our bodies through our senses, electrochemical signals are sent through the nervous system to the brain. These signals are similar to electrical currents that power appliances, although the physical processes are different. This information travels through the body before arriving at the language centers of the mind, and we call it life energy.[4] *Energy* is a fitting word for what comes from the heart because it represents formless information that stimulates a potential for action.

The activity in the diagram may begin any time we become aware of our conversation. Since NVC is about developing awareness in OFNR, the place in the diagram where we start does not matter. NVC is usually taught in the order of the acronym OFNR, and so we begin the discussion with observation.

The OFNR Process and Self-Empathy

The following numbered items explain the activities in the state diagram of Figure 1. Each gives an example of what our internal dialogue could sound like when going through a process of self-empathy.

1. One of the very first steps we can take to begin developing our observation skills and self-empathy is to ask ourselves, *What am I thinking?* For example, during a conversation with a friend, I might be making a judgment about someone else, such as, *Frank doesn't know what he's doing.*

2. After becoming aware of our thoughts, and perhaps writing them down, we ask ourselves, *What am I feeling?* and *What do I need?* The heart, a metaphor for our truest self, is constantly alive, whether we're aware of it or not. It has the essential information about our current life experience, encompassing our senses and internal

needs, including physical, personal, interpersonal, and transcendent needs.

3. After asking ourselves what we're feeling and needing, we listen for the answer, which is shown in the diagram as our life energy.

4. Our mind then translates this heart information into words. Part of the value of NVC is to help us create a lexicon of words about feelings and needs to describe more accurately what we're experiencing inside. The words representing feelings and needs are labels that we put on different experiences and sensations. The purpose of the words is to be clear and to communicate our experience to other people. For example, continuing internal our conversation about Frank, the translation might sound like, *I'm feeling frustrated and want more clarity and ease.*

The translation of our experiences into words is not an exact science; it is only an approximation for both the speaker and the listener. Although dictionaries do a thorough job of defining words for common intellectual understanding, they can be inadequate in describing the experiences of the heart. Different people have different definitions and uses for the words they use to describe their feelings and needs; a dialogue about what we mean by the heart words we use supports clarity and connection. There are times when the words can get in the way of connecting with others. When our goal is mutual understanding, we strive for clarity in our choice of words we use to describe our experiences.

5. There is usually some thinking involved in the translation, and it is easy to get stuck in the thinking. NVC counsels us to move quickly into the request.

6. The final stage of awareness in NVC is to decide on a request to make, either to ourselves or to someone else. We might even make this request of God through prayer. The request is what helps us get our needs met, for our needs are a gift from God, to whom I might say, *God, please help me! None of this makes sense!* To Frank, I might say "Excuse me — I'm confused and I need a little clarity. Would you be willing to tell me what you mean by ____?"

Sadly, over time we may get disconnected from our hearts, which happens when we judge ourselves, believe other people's judgments, and don't inquire into our needs. We end up spending an unbalanced amount of time in our minds believing the judgments and experiencing unpleasant feelings. These periods of time can be short, as in a few seconds, or they can span over several years, and experienced as chapters of desolation and depression in our lives. Our goal in this book is to shorten the period of time that it takes to reconnect with our hearts; the Holy Spirit does the rest.

When we take the time to learn how to honor and protect this amazing and vital connection to our own heart, we eventually experience a life filled with peace and joy. The tools in this book will help you recover that connection to your heart and find better relationships with the people in your life, be they intimate connections, workplace relationships, friendships, or familial bonds; relationships in small groups, with teachers or students, in health care, law enforcement, or governance. In short, it applies to any situation in which people interact and communicate with each other.

For those of you who consider yourselves Christian, whether Catholic, Protestant, Evangelical or another denomination, you will learn new ways of putting foundational Christian principles into practice and gain a deeper connection and intimacy with God and others. Of course, everyone else is also invited into this conversation.

2.

Christ Integration

Jesus said to the people who believed in him, "You are truly my disciples if you remain faithful to my teachings." (John 8:31, NLT)

Christ integration is a journey with the destination of a life faithfully lived in harmony with the Gospels. In my experience, following and living out the message of Jesus brings healing and fulfillment through which I have known a profound sense of joy, awe, and sometimes sadness—all of which have added to the depth of my life's journey. To support the integration with scripture, I quote extensively from the Gospels according to Matthew and John.

In addition to Rosenberg's book on NVC, *Nonviolent Communication: A Language of Life*, I have been influenced and inspired by Brian McLaren's book *The Secret Message of Jesus: Uncovering the Truth that Could Change Everything* and Walter Wink's book *The Powers That Be: Theology for a New Millennium*. After three people independently suggested that I check out Fr. Richard Rohr, I celebrated the synergies as I read his book *Things Hidden: Scripture as Spirituality*. I have also been helped by reading books from Catholic, Protestant, Evangelical, and nonreligious authors such as Joseph Girzone, Thomas Bokenkotter, Clarissa Pinkola Estés, Anthony de Mello, Thomas Moore, Melody Beattie, Dallas Willard, Elaine Pagels, Larry Crabb, John Eldredge, Frank Viola, Mike Erre, Henry Cloud, and John Townsend.

In light of these inspiring books, mine is unique because I integrate the teachings of Jesus with NVC, resulting in a practical-conversational spirituality. As such, it can be seen as supporting *spiritual formation* in the growth and development of the whole person by focusing on

- The spiritual and interior life,
- Interactions with others in ordinary life, and
- Spiritual practices such as prayer, the study of scripture, fasting, simplicity, solitude, confession, and worship.[5]

For Evangelicals, spiritual formation can be seen as sanctification in a new key, as pointed out by Steve Porter.[6] In short, conversation and the way I approach it is part of my spiritual practice — a discipline of love in conversation.

This book is less about doctrine than about living out Jesus's values and their underlying principles and those placed in our hearts by our creator. It's about living in integrity with ourselves so that our insides match our outsides. This is not counseling or therapy. It's an invitation to participate in and share the loving, creative expression of the heart of God, out of which we were created and whose image and likeness we share. It's about empowering people and teaching them how to have intimate, more fulfilling conversations and loving relationships.

I quote almost exclusively the words attributed to Jesus because I am inspired by them and because they contain timeless wisdom. I explain my interpretations in light of my experience and my understanding of the Gospel and how it can help us communicate in loving ways consistent with our Christian values. I am not interested in making theological proofs. If you're looking for proofs, please put down this book and save time, money, and disappointment. You must be hungry for connection, interdependence, companionship, community, intimacy, and love with other human beings to get any value from this book.

Each chapter ends with discussion questions to ponder, complemented by occasional exercises. I encourage you to discuss them in a group. My hope is that you too will find clarity and fulfillment by exploring the concepts presented, and will experience for yourself a spirit of love in all your relationships.

3.

Interpersonal Violence

I woke up the other day, tottered to the kitchen for a cup of coffee, and headed to the living room for my daily ritual of reading and writing. Mark, my roommate, appeared out of nowhere and said, "I got sucker punched last night."

Startled, I mumbled, "Huh? What did you say?"

"I got punched and went to the emergency room last night."

My muscles tensed, my breathing got shallow, and my heart rate shot up. He spoke again. "Look! Check out my stitches."

His lower lip was bruised. He turned to the right so I could see the side of his head. It was stitched and stapled with three lines in the shape of a Mercedes logo. "Wow! How did that happen?" I asked.

"I was sitting at the bar watching the Laker game when this guy I used to hang out with walked in and sat down next to me. After a while he asked me why I didn't call him anymore. I told him I don't like the way he treats people. The conversation got heated, and before I knew it, I was on the floor. I opened my eyes and saw people looking down at me, worried. I tried to get up, but they advised me not to. Then I noticed the puddle of blood all around me." He paused for a moment. "Do you have any Tylenol or Advil? I have a headache."

Concerned, I went to the kitchen and got two ibuprofen tablets. As he swallowed them, I told him to eat something so his stomach wouldn't get upset.

"I'm not worried about food," he said. "I'm going back to bed."

As the day progressed, I found my thoughts wandering back to Mark and what had happened. After I thought about it, I realized I was afraid for my own safety. My thoughts went something like this: *The attacker is probably part of a gang. They're going to come over and torch the place. Or maybe they'll just shoot their way inside and then torch the place. I better keep my cell phone close by. I wonder what kind of defenses I could prepare.* Then I started thinking about my son. *I'm glad Alex isn't here this week.*

My mind was spinning with ideas on how to protect myself. At one point, I thought about striking up a conversation with the attacker. Then I realized I had more questions. I felt the need for safety and protection and wanted more information from Mark.

That evening, I asked Mark to tell me more about what happened. In my living room, I got to hear more of the story. At one point in the conversation, I kindly interrupted him and said, "Mark, I've got some stuff coming up for me. Is it all right if I tell you?"

"Yeah, sure." He appeared concerned. I wondered if he was thinking I might be judging him.

I said, "I'm feeling scared, as if my own safety were at stake. I see you as part of my family; we came from the same God and we share a common ancestry. You're like a brother to me."

Mark nodded. I went on, "I'm also angry that this would happen. A part of me wants justice, because he might do it again. Do you know if he's done this before?"

"Yes," Mark admitted. "He's done it many times, and that's one of the reasons I didn't want to hang out with him in the first place. Funny thing is, that's exactly what we were arguing about before he hit me. I was telling him that I didn't like how he treated people, and then, wham! I woke up in a puddle of blood."

I asked if he thought it could happen again with other people. He said yes.

"Mark, I know this is about you, but I want you to know that it's also about me. A part of me feels pain and concern for my safety. I think you'd be doing everybody a favor by intervening in this guy's life and taking a stand for justice."

Mark seemed to take in my point. Then he said: "I'm thinking about pressing charges. I'm tired. I'm going to bed."

This story is about just one manifestation of violence, and it points out the challenge of finding ways to achieve mutual understanding that results in peace.

Violence doesn't have to be physical. It can and does happen through the words that we speak to others and to ourselves. It can happen subtly, when people seek to get their needs met at the expense of others.

For example, if I say, "You're stupid," I'm being violent with my words. In the extreme, the judgments that we make completely separate us from our hearts, as shown in Figure 2.

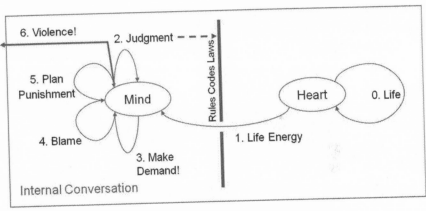

Figure 2. Disconnected Heart State Diagram

This is the extreme case in which a person doesn't have a language of feelings and needs and is stimulated by something uncomfortable. The following examples summarize what the thinking behind each of the activities represented by the arrows could sound like in a circumstance that is unpleasant, but does not involve physical violence.

0. Life goes on whether the mind is aware or not. The heart beats; we breathe, eat, sleep, and go about our lives.

As we interact with our environment, our heart is stimulated by it through our senses.

1. The heart sends out life energy that is picked up by the mind. The heart stimulates the mind regardless of whatever thinking goes on. Feelings associated with the stimulus could be hurt, anger, anxiety, or fear.

2. Without the reference point of a language of feelings and needs, the mind makes a judgment of what it thinks is the cause of discomfort, usually someone else. It looks outside to a set of rules, codes, or laws as a point of reference. We might think something like, *You incompetent bastard!*

3. This person makes a demand of someone. *I want you to do it my way or else!*

4. If the other person doesn't comply perfectly with the demand, they're blamed for the discomfort and unpleasantness that might follow. *It's your fault, you idiot!*

5. The mind continues the blame-game by exploring ways in which to punish the other person. The thought might be very direct. *You deserve to be punished!*

6. The aggrieved person either delivers the punishment right away or passive-aggressively stores it away for a more effective time. This leads to violence for both parties. *I'll get you later, when it will hurt more.*

Sometimes the sequence happens very quickly from event to stimulus to violence because the violent reaction has been reinforced over time.

4.

Admitting We Have a Societal Problem

I'm afraid of delving too deeply into the problems we have as a society. My fear is that if I give them too much attention, they will detract from the message I want to contribute. Instead of getting lost in specific examples of our societal problems, which could fill a book on their own, I focus instead on some evaluations of the problems. I do this on behalf of my needs for clarity, flow, and efficient use of words. I hope you can interpolate some specific instances that stimulate these evaluations. If you struggle with doing so, I suggest watching the evening news one night (any night), recording all of the instances of violence, and noticing how you feel as you hear about each one.

My perception is that things are so bad that I have decided to limit my exposure to TV programming. I'm not saying that the news or TV programs are bad or evil, but they contain information regarding the conversations we have as a society and the state of disconnection with our hearts. I am choosing to focus my attention elsewhere.

All of the arguing, posturing, and finger-pointing in Washington have stimulated anger, suspicion, anxiety and frustration. I see violence in much of the public discourse. Then there are the two wars and all the death and suffering they bring. Then there's the collapse and subsequent bailout of the financial system and how a few well-placed individuals brought the world economy to its knees and walked away with a fortune. They got their financial support needs met at the expense of the American people and caused a negative impact that extends worldwide. I am baffled at how politicians would block reform efforts, but then, I know that some have much to gain from the status quo.

Even though I live in a county with a lot of money, I don't have to go far to see the effects of poverty on the quality of life of people who don't have much and the poverty of the soul in some who have more money than they can spend.

Money in itself is not good or evil; it's just a tool for meeting needs. A problem arises when we treat money like a need and we disconnect from the heart, losing our connection with God.[7]

In *Everything Must Change: Jesus, Global Crises, and a Revolution of Hope*, Brian McLaren suggests that we suffer from four deep dysfunctions.

1. *Prosperity Crisis*. Environmental breakdown caused by our unsustainable global economy, an economy that fails to respect environmental limits even as it succeeds in producing great wealth for about one-third of the world's population.

2. *Equity Crisis*. The growing gap between the ultrarich and the extremely poor, which prompts the poor majority to envy, resent, and even hate the rich minority, which in turn elicits fear and anger in the rich.

3. *Security Crisis*. The danger of cataclysmic war arising from the intensifying resentment and fear among various groups at opposite ends of the economic spectrum.

4. *Spiritual Crisis*. The failure of the world's religions, especially its two largest religions, Christianity and Islam,[8] to provide a framing story capable of healing or reducing the other three crises.

I agree with McLaren that the fourth of these is the leverage point for healing the first three; this book addresses the spiritual crisis by applying the teachings of Jesus in the practical conversational framework of NVC.

McLaren identifies the most crucial global problems, which I translate into the following societal needs not being adequately met: safety, justice, education, equality, environmental and personal health, peace, stability, financial support, and fairness. With awareness of our needs and a connection to our hearts, we begin to feel a natural desire to reform the system so that it can support the needs and values of the people it's intended to serve. This typically results in a strategy of transforming the governments so that they serve the needs of their people in equitable, open, and transparent ways.

In *The Powers That Be*, Walter Wink points out the following about the collective spirit of human institutions, which he calls the Powers.

The Powers are good.
The Powers are fallen.
The Powers must be redeemed. [9]

5.

Redeeming the Societal Collective

Redemption is not something that we can do ourselves or demand from God. We could sit back in despair, blame others, continue to follow the path we're on, or we could choose to follow the teachings of Jesus in our path toward God, accepting his grace, seeing the truth of our experience, connecting to others, and listening for the Holy Spirit's guidance in finding strategies for meeting everyone's needs. Once we have an awareness of needs, we can begin to have a dialogue about how getting our needs met at the expense of others is missing the heart of God. We can also talk about meeting someone else's needs at the expense of our own. Both of these are forms of violence, also known as sin.

It is through the collective efforts at connecting through our hearts, embracing the wisdom already there, and spurring action from those awake enough to be the change they want that human institutions will be redeemed. Through this conversation of the heart and mind, we can taste the soul and strength from the living water of Christ. We begin to do things not out of duty, obligation, legal requirements, or to buy someone's love, but with integrity because it brings us joy to participate in the banquet of life. We find our place at the table with our larger family of humanity, with Jesus smiling and passing the bread and wine around the table.

This is the journey to which you are invited in this book. I hope that at the very least, it will stimulate lots of dialogue about the nature of conversation and how Christ is alive, well, and present in our lives if we choose to let him in.

This book addresses the societal spiritual crisis by showing that Jesus's message can help us reframe our conversations and bring about deeper connection and intimacy with others. We can recover our hearts, both individually and collectively.

My hypothesis is that by healing our hearts and learning ways to communicate in which everyone's needs are considered, we'll find a path that leads to solving our problems; I wouldn't be surprised if we also experience some joy along the way toward peace. This book is about empowering individuals with the tools to connect. The good news is that Jesus has been pointing us in that direction for a couple of millennia.

6.

The Good News

The solution to our problems lies much closer to home than in Washington and all the other capitals in the world. It resides in the space that is closer to the heart.

Our natural tendency, when presented with a stressful situation, is to fight, flee, or freeze.[10] More often than not, I have chosen to fight instead of flee. My experience tells me that everyone suffers when I choose violence—when I choose to sin.

Jesus presents us with a new option to transcend these tendencies.[11] He invites us to connect to his spirit, offer the grace we've received, listen to others through love, speak our truth in love, and find new ways to address our current challenges. In fact, he said that he would send us a counselor to help us who is available to us *now*.[12] We just need to be willing to let go of our worldly strategies and engage each other in a heartfelt conversation, discovering the truth of our collective experience. He is inviting us to a life fully lived in his presence and to experience the commonality of humanity through love. And to be invited to a banquet of the spirit is for me a glorious opportunity not to be missed.[13]

II.

ECHOES OF THE GARDEN

What is judgment? This section defines judgment and discusses its effects on our ability to relate to each other, to God, and to ourselves. The word *judgment* has several meanings. We'll discuss two: value judgments and moral judgments.

1. *Value judgments* tell us whether needs and values are being satisfied by means of self-examination.[14] Determining if one's needs are being met is part of the process of self-empathy, or clarifying which feelings and needs are currently being stimulated. We experience pleasant feelings when needs are met, and unpleasant feelings when needs are not met.

2. *Moral judgments* refer to the rules of right and wrong or good and evil.[15] Moral judgment results from believing that we have the knowledge and power of God and the role of a judge. This is a direct result of eating from the Tree of Knowledge of Good and Evil, which I sometimes call the Tree of Judgment.

Take note that the source of information for a moral judgment lies outside us. When we make value judgments, we look inside ourselves for the source of information. This distinction is important and will be revisited many times in this book. The word *judgment* is most commonly used to mean moral judgment. In this book, the word *judgment* will mean *moral judgment* unless stated otherwise.

7.

A Personal Story of Judgment

When I first moved to Orange County, I attended a large nondenominational Christian church after my neighbor invited me to a swing dance hosted there. I made many friends and dove into a lot of activities almost simultaneously.

Within a week, my calendar was filled with events, and I was spending time with people I hadn't known just a few short weeks before. Clearly, there was something in my heart that resonated with this community. This went on for several years.

At one point, I started dating someone I met in the Bible study. While dating, we experienced joy and happiness, as well as hurt, sadness, frustration, and anger as we played out our unmet needs from childhood. We dated on and off for four years. My needs for connection and intimacy were met while the relationship was on, but it was at the expense of my own needs for safety, stability, and self-respect. I was disconnected from my heart and not fully aware of my needs. I focused on meeting her needs at the expense of my own.

We joined a small group of people who met weekly to mutually support each other's spiritual growth.

One day, after reconnecting with my girlfriend at the beginning of another *on* period, I still did not have the commitment and stability I wanted, yet I was back in the relationship. So I acted out by, going on a lunch date with someone else. In the back of my mind, I was hoping that my girlfriend would find out. She did, and this eventually broke us up for good.

We agreed to bring the issue to the small group. I was expecting an honest dialogue around both of our perspectives, but instead I experienced a lot of judgment. The group members made their own evaluations of what was right and wrong about the things we did. I do have some regret around my actions, because my needs for integrity, respect, and consideration were not met by my own actions. I also mourn that my need for a mutually respectful dialogue that considered both my girlfriend and me was not met. And finally, that the group dynamic didn't support our growth.

Looking back, I now have more clarity about that experience. One lesson I learned is that because I wasn't in tune with my heart and my needs, I built up resentment. My needs for stability and self-respect weren't being met in the relationship. Eventually this led to anger, and I got back at my girlfriend in wacky ways and then shortly after felt guilty about it. I knew I had to change, but I needed acceptance, support, and a lot of empathy if I was to grow. It was around this time that I attended my first NVC nine-day intensive training session, which helped me find the clarity I needed to move forward and get to where I am now: writing a book.

Another key lesson I learned was how my own judgment affected me. I judged my friends for judging me by making them out to be the enemy. I created enemy images of them inside my head; I didn't want to hang out with them or with the wider community anymore; I now see that behind my judgments of them were feelings of sadness and disappointment because my needs for support, and mutual respect were not met. I then projected that same judgment inward on myself. I was trying to live up to a standard of perfection that I myself couldn't achieve. The internal judgment I projected on myself was triggered by my friends, but ultimately the judgments were <u>my own thoughts</u>. They took the form of guilt, shame, and depression. I told myself things like, *I'm misunderstood. I'm no good. I don't belong.*

In my friends' defense, I believe they intended to help me by following their own understanding of what it means to be Christian. What I realized was that while I wanted to grow, my growth was not helped by this type of group dynamic. I realized that I needed an environment of acceptance and love to support the journey that lay before me. I needed the freedom to walk my own path with acceptance of who I was as a person and the support to help me clarify the life strategies that weren't serving me, my girlfriend, or the greater good. I now realize that I needed more empathy than my friends were able or willing to offer at the time.

Now that time has passed and healing has taken place, I'm grateful for those friendships and what I learned from them. As a result, I've taken steps to reconnect with these old friends.

8.

The Stupid, Evil Squirrel

Judgments have nothing to do with the person, place, or thing being judged and everything to do with the person doing the judging. Judgments adversely affect the judge, even when the object of our judgment is a squirrel.

One morning, while enjoying a hot cup of coffee with a close friend and reading the morning newspaper, I looked out at her backyard covered with snow. As I peered out the window, enjoying the expanse of green and white, I noticed a squirrel approaching the house. Suddenly I heard my friend say, "That stupid squirrel — it's evil!"

Startled and no longer enjoying the beauty of the outdoors, I pondered my response to my friend's outburst. I was alarmed, then annoyed. I began to relax once I connected with my needs for peace that weren't being met in the moment. After a few minutes, I began to get curious about my friend's statement about the squirrel; I was totally confused because I didn't know why she called the squirrel evil and stupid. I wanted to help my friend see how her judgment affected us, I just wasn't clear how.

I worried that if I spoke up about my feelings, she would hear them as criticisms, so I let it go. Later that afternoon, I tried to express how I felt about something completely unrelated, but she began interpreting my words as a judgment of her, and that led to a total breakdown of our connection and left me feeling frustrated and her feeling hurt.

We both needed a timeout, so we went to an outdoor jogging track. After sprinting a mile, I returned to the car for a nap while my friend completed her workout. When we got home, I requested some time alone with her in the kitchen. We sat down at the table and I let her know that I wanted to share something with her, but I was worried that she would hear it as a judgment. I asked if she was interested in hearing what I had to say, and she said yes.

"Lesley," I said, "I'm concerned about your response to the squirrel this morning. Would you like to hear how I felt about that?"

"Yes," she replied with a worried look on her face.

"I heard you call the squirrel stupid and evil."

I guessed that Lesley was afraid of judgment, so I tried to convey a desire to connect using my tone of voice and body posture. "I'm worried that you're trapped in a box of judgment and I want to contribute to your freedom." I paused for a moment and then said, "Would you be willing to tell me what you heard me say?"

Lesley said, "You're worried and want to contribute to my freedom?"

"Yes," I said. "I'm wondering if you could tell me more about what goes on with you regarding the squirrel because I'm confused by your response. What's behind calling the squirrel stupid and evil?"

Lesley explained, "That damn squirrel digs up my plants in the spring, eats up all the birdseed, and makes a mess in the yard. I'm afraid he'll dig a nest in our home, bite into an electrical wire, and cause a fire."

That was three reasons in quick succession before I could give her any empathy, so I picked the last one on her list. "So you're afraid and want to keep your house safe?" I asked.

"Yes," she said, "and I have to spend a lot of time in the spring replanting my flowers after the squirrel digs them up."

"Are you feeling annoyed because you want more ease and less effort and to protect the beauty of your garden?"

"Yes," she said. "It's a lot of work to plant and replant the flowers."

"So you'd like some acknowledgment for the effort it takes to replant the flowers?" I responded.

"Yes."

I noticed that her body posture was starting to relax as her explanations got shorter and her voice became quieter. I wanted all her concerns to be addressed, so I pressed on.

"Are you also feeling annoyed when you see the birdseed shells scattered around the feeder because you want more beauty and order in your backyard?"

"Yes," she said, almost in tears. I guessed that she had received enough empathy for now. I paused for a moment, watching her, and asked, "Would you like to know what went on for me when I heard you calling the squirrel stupid and evil?"

"Sure!" she said enthusiastically.

I said, "Lesley, when I hear you call the squirrel stupid and evil I get scared that the same judgment you use on the squirrel will get turned toward me, and I really long for mutual acceptance, especially with close friends." I took a breath and went on. "Would you be willing to tell me what I just said?"

"That you're afraid of my judgment?" she said. I noticed that she heard what I didn't want instead of hearing what I did want. She was only hearing part of my response.

"Thanks," I said. "That was close. I really want you to hear that I want mutual consideration and acceptance—that I want you to value my needs as much as yours. Those are the needs behind my own fear of judgment. Would you be willing to tell me that?"

Lesley seemed to be hearing me better now. "So, you want acceptance and you're afraid of judgment?"

"Yes. Thank you. I also want you to know that I felt some sadness because I lost connection with you. Would you be willing to tell me that?" I said.

"That you're feeling sad because you lost connection with me?"

"Thanks. How do you feel at hearing me say that?" I asked.

"Gosh, I had no idea all this was going on," she said. "I'm especially sad that we lost connection. I know I have a tendency to judge, but I didn't know how it affected others."

After recognizing that we had a common understanding of our experience, I turned our attention to the squirrel to complete the story.

"Lesley, what do you think is motivating the squirrel to do the things it does?" I asked.

Lesley and I explored how the squirrel was getting its needs met. It buried nuts underneath the plants to protect them from the cold and save them for later—meeting its need for security. The squirrel was eating the birdseed because it was hungry—meeting its need for sustenance. And the squirrel occasionally digs into homes to build its shelter. Lesley saw that she had some things in common with that squirrel.

I sensed that we had a full connection and deeper understanding, given that both of us spoke about our needs and what came up for us in that situation. We also practiced giving empathy to the squirrel when we guessed what its needs were.

This story demonstrates the cost of judgment and how empathy and honesty can be used to uncover the truth behind it. Lesley was so used to judging others and herself that it was second nature. Her negative evaluations of herself not only affected how she saw and experienced the world, but also how she saw and experienced herself. I found it difficult to have a balanced conversation with her because she interpreted the expression of my unpleasant feelings as criticism and judgment.

I hope the story of my experience with Lesley and the squirrel illustrates the negative effects that judgment can have on our relationships. The story isn't about the squirrel; it's about how Lesley interpreted, labeled, and judged the squirrel's actions.

Discussion

- Have you ever experienced a time when you were enjoying something and were interrupted? Describe what happened.
- Can you identify with Lesley in the story? If so, how?
- Were you touched by the story? If so, at what point?
- How often do you see judgment in your daily life? Is it easy to see, or are you used to it and don't notice it?
- Why do you think judgment is so prevalent in our world?

9.

The Tree of Knowledge of Good and Evil

I assume that most of us have heard the story of Adam and Eve in the Garden of Eden. When I was little, I believed that because of the actions by Adam and Eve I was doomed to live in a world of sin and there was nothing I could do about it. Today, as I look more closely at my life—my actions, motivations, and beliefs—I'm rethinking the meaning of this story.

The Invitation to Live in the Garden

> *Now the Lord God had planted a garden in the east, in Eden; and there he put the man he had formed. And the Lord God made all kinds of trees grow out of the ground—trees that were pleasing to the eye and good for food. In the middle of the garden were the tree of life and the tree of the knowledge of good and evil.*
>
> *The Lord God took the man and put him in the Garden of Eden to work it and take care of it. And the Lord God commanded the man, "You are free to eat from any tree in the garden; but you must not eat from the tree of the knowledge of good and evil, for when you eat of it you will surely die."* (Genesis 2:8–9, 15–17, NIV)

I chose these verses to focus on the issues related to the tree. I am struck by the fact that Adam and Eve were free to eat from any tree except one: the Tree of Knowledge of Good and Evil.[16] God warned them of the dangers of eating from that tree.[17] After they ate its fruit, Adam and Eve were expelled from the Garden of Eden, and their communion with God was lost.

God could have prevented Adam and Eve from eating from the tree if that's what he wanted. He could have

- Created a moat with alligators around the tree
- Put walls of cacti around it
- Hidden it in some distant corner of the Garden
- Made it invisible to the human eye
- Not created the tree in the first place
- Created human automatons without a free will.

Okay, I had a little fun considering some options to make a point. God could have done any of these things, but he didn't. He did the following.

- He created the Tree of Knowledge of Good and Evil.
- He made it pleasing to the eye.
- He put it in the middle of the Garden, where Adam and Eve would surely see it.
- He created Adam and Eve with

  - Curiosity and thirst for knowledge.
  - Hunger for food.
  - The ability to communicate with each other and with him.
  - The ability to make their own choices based on information.
  - The ability to process information through dialogue with God and each other.

I often wonder what would have happened if Adam and Eve had used all the gifts at their disposal instead of just one or two. If they had chosen to process their information together and even consult with God in the matter, things could have been a lot different. In an imaginary dialogue, I refer to God by a translation of the name Jesus used for his Father: *Abba*, a term of endearment usually translated as *Daddy*. Adam and Eve enjoyed intimate communion with God, and they would call him *Abba* out of affection. The dialogue might have sounded something like this.

Eve: "Hey, Adam, would you come over here?"

Adam: "Huh? Oh, all right. What's up?"

Eve: "Have you ever seen a tree like this? Look at those shallow roots and the trunk and how richly brown and thin they are. And the branches, they look kind of like your arms after you've spent the day throwing boulders into the lake. And the leaves — they're so brown and yet alive, they seem to glow in the daylight. And check out those bright beautiful apples ... Adam, did you hear anything I said?"

Adam: "Uh, yeah. I heard all of it. Great tree, huh?"

Eve: "Would you be willing to listen to me for the next fifteen minutes? I have a hunch it could save you lots of effort, and it might save me some pain!"

Adam: "Okay, Eve. Sorry, I'm just having a lot of fun here. I'll listen to you for fifteen minutes, and then I'll check in. Um, what's a minute again?"

Eve: "Forget the minute thing! I'm drawn to that beautiful apple. That pushy snake over there tells me that if I eat it my eyes will be opened and I'll be like God."

Adam: "Eve, are you nuts? Those serpents are always trying to sell you something we don't need. And Daddy said not to eat it. He said something like, 'You will surely die!' Don't you remember?"

Eve: "Yeah, I remember something like that. But the serpent says our eyes will be opened and we'll see the Garden the way God sees it."

Adam: "Eve, I've got a bad feeling about this. In fact, I'm feeling a tightening in my stomach and my breathing is getting fast and shallow."

Adam sneezes. "Achoo!"

Eve: "You're feeling 'anxious'?"

41

Adam: "Yeah, we'll call that 'anxious.' I'm feeling anxious because I love Daddy, and I'm afraid of losing him."

Eve: "So you're scared of losing Daddy's love?"

Adam: "Yes!"

Eve: "But the apple is so pretty! The snake says now is the season for it and tomorrow it might be gone."

Serpent: "Hey, lady! We're burning daylight here. Do you want the apple or not?"

Adam: "Eve, I hear you really want the apple. It's very pretty. I'm also curious about that tree and what the serpent is claiming. I love you and I love our Father too. Why don't we take a break, go for a walk in the Garden, and ask Daddy what he thinks?"

Eve: "Gosh, Adam, I really enjoyed hearing what you said. I'm feeling warm and cuddly inside. Okay, let's go for a walk and talk about it."

Adam: "Thanks for hearing me. I'm feeling warm and cuddly too. Let's go play on the top of the hill. Daddy said to multiply—I don't know what he meant, but it sounds fun, doesn't it?"

Eve: "Yeah, that does sound fun!" Eve takes off running.

Adam turns back to the serpent: "Nice try, slimy!"

Adam runs after Eve …

Now that's an interesting conversation. Eve consults with Adam and they decide to go play instead. The story implies that they have the intention to talk to God. But it's interesting to note that they also used the gifts God had given them at creation: curiosity, communication skills, making choices consistent with their values.

Discussion

- Can you think of other ways the conversation could have gone? How?

- Why do you think God didn't prevent Adam and Eve from eating from the Tree of Knowledge of Good and Evil?

- What are some other ways in which God could have stopped them? Be creative.

- The author makes a list of what God gave to Adam and Eve when he created them. Do you agree with the list? Is there anything missing?

- How did you experience the dialogue in this chapter? What feelings are coming up for you? Do you know why?

- What is the result of eating from the Tree of Knowledge of Good and Evil today—in everyday life? Give specific examples to support your point.

10.

The Birth of Judgment

Now the serpent was more crafty than any of the wild animals the Lord God had made. He said to the woman, "Did God really say, 'You must not eat from any tree in the garden'?"

The woman said to the serpent, "We may eat fruit from the trees in the garden, but God did say, 'You must not eat fruit from the tree that is in the middle of the garden, and you must not touch it, or you will die.'"

"You will not surely die," the serpent said to the woman. "For God knows that when you eat of it your eyes will be opened, and you will be like God, knowing good and evil."

When the woman saw that the fruit of the tree was good for food and pleasing to the eye, and also desirable for gaining wisdom, she took some and ate it. She also gave some to her husband, who was with her, and he ate it. Then the eyes of both of them were opened, and they realized they were naked; so they sewed fig leaves together and made coverings for themselves. (Genesis 3:1–7, NIV)

I am humbled by the rich symbolism in this story. The tree's being in the middle of the garden tells us how easy it is to see and therefore how easy it is to fall into its temptation. Second, the serpent was crafty, remaining hidden most of the time. He showed himself just long enough to plant the seed of the illusion that we will be like God, knowing good and evil. But God at this point didn't say that after eating from the tree that Adam and Eve would actually know good and evil; that was the serpent speaking. God said, "For when you eat of it *you will surely die*" (Gen. 2:17, emphasis added).

After eating from the tree, we would believe ourselves to be judges, having the knowledge of all people, but we wouldn't really possess such knowledge. Ever since then we have lived under the illusion that we have the power to judge and evaluate others. Along with this evaluation comes death. Given that in the rest of the chapter Adam and Eve don't physically die, the message in the story is that something inside them died because they ate from the tree, but they gained something else in its place.

In Genesis 3:7, Adam and Eve realized they were naked. They turned this knowledge of good and evil toward themselves and felt shame and covered their bodies: something within them was not okay anymore. Adam and Eve judged themselves right after eating the fruit. They lost their connection with God, and as a result, a part of them died.

Discussion

- Do you think Adam and Eve would still have eaten the fruit without the serpent? Why or why not?
- Why do you think God made the serpent?
- What does the serpent represent today?

The Effect of Judgment

Then the man and his wife heard the sound of the Lord God as he was walking in the garden in the cool of the day, and they hid from the Lord God among the trees of the garden. But the Lord God called to the man, "Where are you?"

He answered, "I heard you in the garden, and I was afraid because I was naked; so I hid."

And he said, "Who told you that you were naked? Have you eaten from the tree that I commanded you not to eat from?"

The man said, "The woman you put here with me — she gave me some fruit from the tree, and I ate it." (Genesis 3:8–12, NIV)

"I was afraid because I was naked" indicates that one effect of eating from the tree is the fear that we feel when our experience isn't in harmony with something inside us. The something within is referred to as the heart.[18] Your heart has the image of the heart of God within it. That part of you is the gift of life. Adam was exposed and vulnerable emotionally, and his heart knew he acted in a way that was not pleasing to God. "So I hid" is a strategy Adam chose to avoid dealing with the effects of being out of harmony with his heart. His actions led to his missing the basic operating instructions written in his heart,[19] leading to a disconnection from the heart of God; another name for this is sin.

Up until they ate from the tree, Adam and Eve were living in harmony with God, with themselves, and with their surroundings in the Garden. Their hearts were invisible to them because they didn't know any other way to live. It's as if you had been healthy all your life and then ate something that didn't agree with your stomach. You would then be keenly aware of the pain in your abdomen.

It was only after they ate from the Tree of Knowledge of Good and Evil that they experienced separation from their hearts and thus from the heart of God. Before this they had shared an intimate communion with God. It is because of this separation that we now require words to describe the heart space. As we will see, heart-space words are essential to communication because they help us to connect.

Discussion

- Why do you think Adam was afraid of God?
- Have you hidden from an expected outcome? Why did you hide?
- Why do you think blame is so prevalent?
- What is the relationship of blame to judgment?

Squirrel Story Continued

Lesley and I continued to talk at the kitchen table. We discussed what was motivating the squirrel outside her window, and we experienced a sense of connection. I knew she read the Bible every day, so I mentioned something for her to ponder.

"Lesley, do you remember in the book of Genesis when Adam and Eve bit into the apple from the forbidden Tree of Knowledge of Good and Evil?"

She nodded.

"When you cast judgment on the squirrel, you eat of that fruit."

Lesley had a bowl of fruit in the middle of the table. I grabbed a shiny red apple and took a huge bite out of it. "You're playing God with the squirrel, thinking that you have the power to cast judgment. And you also turn that judgment on yourself."

We laughed as I waved the apple around to emphasize my words. She expressed her gratitude to me for helping her see something hidden to her.

Later that day, she looked at the front page of the newspaper and said to herself, "That stupid person, she ..."

Old habits are hard to break. The next day, when she told me about what she had read and her reaction, I asked her if she realized she had called the person in the newspaper stupid. We looked at each other for a moment, and then I said, "It's not about the squirrel."

Lesley's tendency to judge was the common denominator with both the squirrel and the article in the newspaper. The judgment had everything to do with Lesley; the squirrel and the person in the article were just going about their lives. When I spend time with Lesley these days and I hear a judgment, I sometimes invite her back to her heart by saying "It's not about the squirrel. Are you feeling ...?"

Exercise

- Describe the room you're in without judgment, without evaluating what you see, as you might see it through the lens of a video camera. Spend at least five minutes on this exercise and write down your description. Share what you wrote with someone else. Help each other identify judgments in your descriptions.

Extended Metaphor of the Tree of Knowledge of Good and Evil

I enjoy using metaphors because they help me to see past my preconceived ideas and make the journey to a deeper truth much easier. In the Garden, there was one tree whose fruit God said not to eat. The wisdom of the Genesis account continues to be relevant today. Here is an extended metaphor based on the Garden of Eden account.

As we eat from the Tree of Knowledge of Good and Evil, we begin to resemble the tree below, becoming seedlings of the tree as we eat from it—metaphorically speaking. We begin to display similar attributes. We behave in ways consistent with the fruit that we eat, and as we grow tall, we begin to create similar fruit to pass on to others, and the cycle of judgment continues.

Tree of Knowledge of Good and Evil

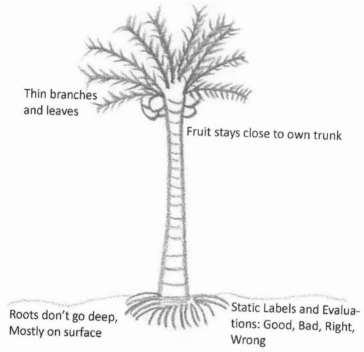

Thin branches and leaves

Fruit stays close to own trunk

Roots don't go deep, Mostly on surface

Static Labels and Evaluations: Good, Bad, Right, Wrong

Judgment is Non-Acceptance.
Don't need Heart, Don't need God

The roots of the Tree of Knowledge of Good and Evil travel horizontally, mostly near the ground, toward other trees. The tree believes the others to be the only source of food. The tree experiences scarcity, thinking it never has enough food, but it has one or two roots that go deep into the soil. These deep roots provide just enough to keep it alive, but the true source of nutrition remains out of reach.

The tree is looking to the other trees for food, but it is not getting enough nourishment. As a result, it blames and criticizes the other trees. The leaves on our tree are mostly brown with thin, short branches.

There is a buildup of internal anger and frustration that our tree uses to put up an illusion of superiority, all the while making judgments of the other trees. It mistakenly believes that by judging the other trees it gets fed, because it feels better momentarily. But the real trickle of nourishment comes to it from deep underground.

Our tree's needs for safety and survival are mistakenly met by its judgment. Its branches are not sufficiently long or strong to reach out to other trees for true connection.

The tree's trunk is narrow. Its branches are thin, and the fruit it bears causes separation and distrust in the forest. It gives off an air of superiority because it is hungry for real food. Unfortunately, it's looking in the wrong place, a place where there is very little food to be had.

The sun also plays a part in our tree metaphor, symbolizing the truth. The tree uses the energy of the sun to criticize others when they don't comply with its own understanding of the truth. The tree has its own set of rules derived from rules it was given. Sadly, our tree also applies the rules to itself, falling short time and time again because it doesn't recognize the real source of nutrients — the source of life in the ground.

As a result, it tragically doesn't get to use or share what it really longs to pull from the depths of its roots. It is never heard, it is not known, and deep inside, it doesn't feel like it fits in with the other trees.

Our tree is always thirsty for the water of empathy, but its internal judge criticizes the clouds for getting it wet. The water does not get a chance to cleanse and comfort the tree, so it is usually feeling sad, hurt, annoyed, and angry and blaming other trees for its thirst. The tree doesn't grow to its potential and is not able to accept simple gifts from others.

The fruit from our tree looks good on the surface. It is very visible at the center of the forest; it is appealing to the eye. Unfortunately, the fruit of our tree has poison that makes one forget that one ate it, making our judgments comfortable and hidden to us. The spirit of judgment takes on a life of its own, nurtured by the fruit; as more and more trees eat the fruit, the poison spreads throughout the forest.

Discussion

- What is the meaning of the Tree of Knowledge of Good and Evil? Do you see this tree as a literal tree that exists somewhere, or do you see it as a metaphor?

- Is the biblical wisdom of the Garden story still relevant today? If so, how?

- Ask yourself if there is there anything you can do today to live more in harmony with the teachings in Genesis, especially about eating the fruit from the Tree of Knowledge of Good and Evil? Write down your answer.

- Does it matter if people continue to eat from the tree? What happens when we eat fruit from this tree today?

- Do I have a choice today to eat or not? If I don't have a choice, what's the implication? If I do have a choice, what's the implication?

Leaving the Garden of Eden—The Fall

And the Lord God said, "The man has now become like one of us, knowing good and evil. He must not be allowed to reach out his hand and take also from the tree of life and eat, and live forever." So the Lord God banished him from the Garden of Eden to work the ground from which he had been taken. After he drove the man out, he placed on the east side of the Garden of Eden cherubim and a flaming sword flashing back and forth to guard the way to the tree of life. (Genesis 3:22–24 NIV)

Adam and Eve's leaving the Garden, which is traditionally called the Fall, has been hard for all of us. God told us that we would die if we ate from the forbidden tree, and we experience that death by our separation from God.

As we play the role of moral judge, a role we were not intended to have, we also experience death in our relationships with others, making it difficult to connect and to find the love for which our hearts were created. We metaphorically continue to eat from the Tree of Knowledge of Good and Evil, and continue to experience separation from our Source, God.

Fast forward several millennia. Jesus came to remind us where we came from and to show us a way back to God—a way back to a loving connection with him, ourselves, and others. And in the richness of metaphorical language, Jesus came to invite us to eat from a vine connected to the Tree of Life, giving us eternal life.

I am the vine; you are the branches. If a man remains in me and I in him, he will bear much fruit; apart from me you can do nothing.... This is to my Father's glory, that you bear much fruit, showing yourselves to be my disciples.... I give them eternal life, and they shall never perish; no one can snatch them out of my hand. (John 15:5, 8, 10:28)

Dr. John Coe writes "this life of moralism, in fact, is what we are saved from: a life of trying to be good and pleasing to

God in the power of the self as a way to deal with our guilt and shame. Rather, the Christian life and spiritual formation are about denouncing the moralistic life."[20]

A common reaction to an awareness of judgment is blind acceptance of all that is around us. Jesus invites us to consider a new way to life that doesn't fall into the extremes of moral judgment and blind acceptance. He invites us into life through a path of love for everyone involved: God, others, and ourselves — to participate in the vine. Jesus invites us into a full integration of the heart and mind,[21] considering both needs and strategies.[22]

God has given us the power to discern something about his truth for us by listening to our hearts without judging others or ourselves as good or evil. Jesus showed us another option. We can discern the truth of our own heart with grace for all involved — this is the Way of Christ. Jesus shows us the way back to God, using something we already have: a heart made in the image and likeness of God.

Discussion

- What is your understanding of the Fall?
- Do you think that individuals have actual knowledge of what is good and what is evil? If so, how do you explain the differences of opinion on the subject? If not, how do you explain that?
- Do you think that God intended for us to have the role of moral judge? Why or why not?
- What are the costs and benefits of judging in your experience? Why do you think you play the role of judge?

11.

We Are Part of the Garden

I find it helpful to remember our roots before the Fall. Adam and Eve lived in perfect harmony with God in the Garden and didn't know any better. After having discussed the impact of eating from the Tree of Knowledge of Good and Evil, it's important to go back to the beginning.

The Image of God in our Hearts

Then God said, "Let us make man in our image, in our likeness, and let them rule over the fish of the sea and the birds of the air, over the livestock, over all the earth, and over all the creatures that move along the ground."

So God created man in his own image, in the image of God he created him; male and female he created them.

God saw all that he had made, and it was very good. And there was evening, and there was morning – the sixth day. (Genesis 1:26–31, NIV)

I am struck by the words *let us make man in our image, in our likeness, both male and female.* There is something of God about us, like us and within us. The word *man* in this context clearly refers to humanity, especially in light of the words *male and female he created them.* It wasn't meant to be a physical image of God, but more the essence of God within us.

These lines in Genesis point to the heart of humanity, the place where the gift of life speaks to us directly. Our hearts speak to us of the motivation and intent of our creation, and we get to experience God through the gift of life that he gave us. Our hearts are good! Actually, God says *all that he made was very good,* and this includes our hearts. At this point in our existence, we lived in constant communion with God, living from our hearts, which were created in his own image.

Jesus came to show us a path back to our hearts, where we are able to love not only our friends, but also our enemies. We need words to help us describe this heart of ours. As we use heart words in conversation, we may recover some of the intimacy we lost in the Fall.

Discussion

- What is your understanding of man being created in the image and likeness of God?

- What comes up for you when you hear that all God made was *very good*? Have you had thoughts about yourself or others that were contrary to this? Explain.

Words that Describe the Heart Space

Above all else, guard your heart, for it is the wellspring of life. (Proverbs 4:23, NIV)

Searching into the depths of my own heart, I discovered a set of words that describe the heart space. In NVC, these words are called *needs* or *values*; I prefer to call them *heart needs*. And while the words themselves are concise labels, they point to a deeper place within us—a place where we can still hear the echoes from the creation of our being.

It's important not to confuse the words with the meaning and the beauty they point to. You have probably heard the saying, "Don't confuse the map with the territory."[23] Eckhart Tolle describes words as pointers to something real. In the case of needs, the words point to something divine within us that we inherited directly from God. Their manifestation in our lives speak to the experience we are having at any one particular moment. The meaning behind each word has existed since the beginning of time, at the dawn of the primordial soup. When God spoke, it all came into being. Greek philosophers called it the *logos*.[24]

At the same time, we must recognize the limitations of language. Words are just the means we use to communicate; the meaning we give to words is important. We must be aware of our definitions, and we need to have images in our mind that connect the labels to something real. The purpose of this chapter is to define some of the words for our heart space—to explore the territory of our hearts so our labels can be pointers on a map of the heart, a sort of compass for connection, enabling love to happen.

Read the following list of heart needs slowly and contemplate your own vision of what the words in italics mean to you; it's important that you have something that authentically works for you. Use what I provide as a starting point. Listen to what the Holy Spirit is saying to you about these things, and write them down in your own notebook.

- *Beauty.* Think about staring into a meadow with a hundred different shades of green. Think of the majesty of ancient pine trees, or the simple rippling sound of a stream of fresh running water. Recall the soothing sound of the waves crashing on the sand at the beach and the green glow of sunlight through a wave just before it breaks. Think about gazing into the center of a rose and smelling its sweet, pungent fragrance.

- *Integrity.* Integrity calls us to act in ways that are consistent with our hearts, ways to live outwardly in harmony with what we know to be true inside. This space within us is stimulated when we see others acting in ways consistent with their values. We are self-similar[25] when we look at our lives in different settings within our various spheres of influence, both internal and external — and they're similar. We authentically behave in ways congruent with our values. Integrity is the opposite of hypocrisy.

- *Contribution.* I have an undeniable desire to contribute to the well-being of my son. The closer I am to God, the more I want to contribute to the well-being of others, and to share an abundant life lived to its fullest. I also enjoy receiving support from others, as they contribute to me. Contribution and support are two sides of giving that are essential to living in community. Sometimes, others are not interested in receiving what I have to offer — I respect their choices, realizing that my contribution would not be a gift unless it is openly received. As I have matured, I discovered my need for a meaningful contribution to the well-being of others; I have sought out my unique gifts, and explore ways in which to offer them.

- *Mutuality.* In a relationship, both people see their needs as important. Our conversations are focused on hearing each other's needs and acknowledging our hearts—we help each other understand what needs are alive, and we routinely reinvent our strategies to connect with those needs. We say to each other, "I value your needs as much as mine and you value my needs just as much as your own." In our relationship, we agree that life is about meeting both of our needs, and we strive to find strategies to meet them. We have a mutual consideration and respect for our unique experiences, and we value equality and balance in what we share.

- *Intimacy.* Remember the conversations that we've had with close friends where we were totally understood and the other person let us know that they were equally understood. Both of our interests and motivations were communicated and treated with utmost value, as if we had discovered radiant diamonds in our life experience and we openly celebrated our new wealth.

- *Belonging.* Being in a group of people who know us, value us, accept us, and celebrate who we are. They encourage us to discover our true selves, to identify gifts, and to follow the paths we deem to be important in accomplishing our life's purpose. We are able to be ourselves, think for ourselves, and speak for ourselves without being pressured to comply with someone else's beliefs. We are known and accepted.

- *Autonomy.* We have the freedom to choose and to make choices that suit us best. Autonomy isn't about living alone on an island but about having the comfort of honestly expressing our personal truth to another person—not at the expense of their needs or our own, but within an open dialogue. We resist any real or perceived pressure to comply with someone else's requests or demands if they don't work for us. We exercise our freedom to choose within a relationship.

- *Clarity.* I was reminded recently of my experience driving over a hill after a heavy rain and clearly seeing the majesty of snow-capped mountains that were normally hidden by smog. I could see farther than I had before. Our need for clarity is met when we fully understand another person and what they're saying because we reflect what we hear, and the other person confirms our understanding. Clarity can also occur within us. We see the world as it is, transcending any pain we may have felt in reaction to an event. We can integrate our thoughts and experiences because they're consistent. Our understanding is refined through requests for more information, by further observation, or through empathy.

- *Connection.* We know and are known. We experience a connection with someone when we share empathy and honesty. If we connect effortlessly, then we can experience Intimacy.

- *Empathy.* Our need for empathy is met when someone is present, when they listen and care about what we say. They might use words to check in and see if they're hearing our heart. Empathy helps us get clear with our current experience, and we begin to feel peace, compassion, and curiosity.

- *Honesty.* Our need for honesty is met when we are able to express to someone our experience and have them let us know they're hearing what we intend to say. We may ask them to tell us what they heard, just to make sure they understood the heart of what we intended. We express honesty without blaming or giving undue credit to someone else for our experience, even though we may be mourning needs not met. We experience freedom as our need for honesty is met.

- *Ease.* Our need for ease is met when things fall into place with little effort. The conversation seems to flow and we lose track of time.

- *Celebration.* We celebrate when our heart is full, when we recognize the beauty in our experience, or when our needs are being met. We celebrate the gift of life that resides within us as a gift from God. As we celebrate, sometimes we invite others to join us and other times we celebrate alone and with God. Sometimes our celebration takes the form of prayer, worship, or singing and dancing. Other times we feel like hugging and kissing our friends or otherwise expressing our gratitude for people's actions.

- *Mourning.* We mourn when some of our needs aren't being met. Perhaps someone has passed on, we might be out of work, or we might be hungry or cold. We might feel sad, longing for our heart to be filled; we might need to be acknowledged. Sometimes we mourn alone. I find great satisfaction in mourning with people who know me and care for me. As our need for mourning is met, we begin to remember the original gift of our heart. The place in our heart that longs for fulfillment is telling us something beautiful about God. As we connect with that hunger within us, we more clearly hear the voice of God telling us something about this moment in time and our place within it. As we recall the original purpose of our heart, we may begin to experience a shift toward joy. Mourning, if given enough time and space to speak its message, turns into celebration as we acknowledge and value it.

- *Meaning* is a word that points deeply into our heart, which celebrates when things come together in unexpected ways. Our need for meaning is met when we are able to contribute to something bigger than ourselves. Our purpose is a specific way in which meaning speaks to our reason for being on the planet. It reminds us of the celestial celebration of our coming into being and of the gifts we have to contribute.

Everyone has their own definition of these words based on their experience and background. It's helpful to remember that the words are just labels for a deeper part of us that we all share because we come from the same God and were created in his image.

In the following list of needs, explore which words speak to your experience today. Take a moment to write a short paragraph about each one and share what you write with someone. It's a simple way to experience a deeper connection with another person.

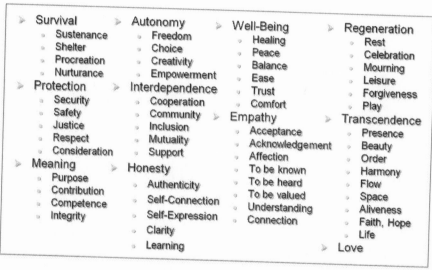

Figure 3. Heart Needs and Values

The heart-space words in Figure 3 can be called heart needs, values, or just needs. They seek expression in order to sustain and enrich life—a life lived to its fullest. There are four main types of needs: survival, personal, interdependent, and transcendent.

We experience pleasant feelings such as joy, happiness, awe, and gratitude when our needs are met. We experience unpleasant feelings such as sadness, fear, annoyance, and anger when our needs are not met. Feelings are neither good nor bad; they're just telling us whether our needs are being met—they just contain information.

It is not surprising to me that the word *need* has such a negative connotation in our culture (e.g., "She needs a lot of attention" or "Don't be so needy"). What is important to remember is that these need words point back to the gift of life—they are the labels we use to describe the things required for life. If we don't get our needs met, we soon die or, at best, go through life all unseeing. A friend recently pointed out to me that sometimes when our needs are not met, over time, we try to kill the longing to have them met.

Heart-space words are important in helping us express our experiences. It's necessary to talk about what happens internally to us and others when heart needs are not met in order to avoid casting blame. Expressing our needs communicates a sense of responsibility for our experience. Many times I feel the urge to blame someone for my "unpleasant" experience. In light of the Fall resulting from eating from the Tree of Knowledge of Good and Evil, I have a tendency to label others as evil or bad when something isn't going well for me.

As a Christian, before I became aware of my needs, I put people in the sinner category if they didn't live in the way I deemed to be right. I now see that as a judgment of others and that I've taken a huge bite from the fruit of the Tree of Knowledge of Good and Evil. When I cast judgment, my loving connection with a person suffers. Sometimes the death is slow; other times it is instantaneous. Not only are my needs for connection and harmony not met as I judge them, but I may cause further harm to others when I think of them as sinners. The harm could take the form of violent speech or actions, which won't meet their needs for respect, consideration, and mutuality. Because of the effects from eating from the Tree of

Knowledge of Good and Evil are moral judgments, I often call it the Tree of Judgment.

Discussion

- Are there any items on the list of needs that you've never experienced? Explain.

- Sometimes our heart needs are met and sometimes they are not met. Are you able to see beauty in them either way? Why or why not?

- Which of the needs and values above have been stimulated for you lately? How? Share your story with someone.

Extended Metaphor of the Tree of Life

Continuing the extended metaphor started earlier, we consider the Tree of Life and some of the symbolism associated with it. As we eat from the Tree of Life, metaphorically, we begin to resemble it.

Tree of Life

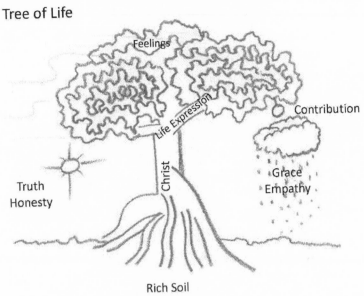

Rich Soil
Acceptance
Source Inheritance of Needs
Heart of God

The soil represents the Heart of God in the form of needs; it provides the key nutrients for the life of the tree. The roots go deep into the soil of our Source inheritance. Love motivates the nutrients from the soil to be available to the roots of the tree; the root's hunger for love and nourishment causes it to absorb the nutrients and transport them up the tree.

Healthy trees get most of their nutrients directly from the soil, giving other trees nearby plenty of space to feed themselves.

The sun gives out the light of truth, which is warm, revitalizing and energizing. The tree captures it with its leaves, propelling the tree to growth through honest expression. The rain is empathetic with the tree, providing a soothing, gentle caress, which cools the tree when it gets too hot, cleans the dust from the leaves, quenches the tree's thirst, and gracefully moistens the nutrients in the soil, allowing them to be captured by the roots. The light of truth and the empathy of the water work together with the earth to support the life and growth of the tree.

The color of the leaves represents feelings and shows whether needs are being met. Greener trees are satisfied, as many of their needs are met. A healthy tree has mostly green leaves. Brown leaves indicate some needs not being met. The brown leaves eventually fall to the ground, turning into compost for future nourishment and growth. The branches grow stronger as needs are acknowledged and fed. They grow long enough to extend themselves to other trees, creating the canopy of community.

Every now and then, a branch turns brown and falls to the ground. This is for the good of the tree, as it enables it to send nutrients to healthier branches, allowing it to grow taller and stronger. At some point in the life of a mature tree, it bears fruit. The fruit symbolizes a contribution to the well-being of the forest, especially the surrounding trees. The taste, shape, and color of the fruit of each tree are unique. This fruit may be a source of food for animals and its seeds a source from which other trees sprout. Eventually, all fruit ripens and falls to the ground, where it becomes food for animals and other trees.

As the tree matures, the quantity of fruit produced diminishes, but the quality and taste improve. As time passes after the tree produces much fruit, it eventually falls, giving its whole self back to the ground that nourished it. The body of the tree is representative of the wisdom accumulated throughout its lifetime. The leaves, branches, trunk, and roots decay slowly, becoming food for other trees in the forest. The tree's decomposition makes room for other trees to grow; new light and water break through the canopy of the forest.

12.

We Can Choose Not to Eat from the Tree of Judgment

In revisiting the Garden story, it's important to acknowledge that we have always had the power to choose. While it is true that Adam and Eve and many of our ancestors ate—and we ourselves continue to eat—from the Tree of Judgment, we can choose not to continue this error and thus move closer to God and other human beings.

Acceptance is a prerequisite for love and is the opposite of judgment. When considering one's own self-acceptance, we need to know at a deep level that God is happy with how we were made. It's important to realize, however, when considering others, that acceptance does not imply agreement with their thoughts or behavior. Acceptance is about allowing others to have their own experiences, behavior and opinions and being okay with it. We might notice that someone's actions may not have met our needs, and could think of more effective strategies, but we don't judge the person as "good" or "bad"; we allow them to remind us of who God made us to be, having been created in his image.

Acceptance of Others

1. Enables us to meet people where they are as opposed to where we'd like them to be.
2. Meets each person's need for mutual respect, autonomy, and freedom to be themselves.
3. Helps us to connect with others.

Judging others isn't *bad*; it just doesn't contribute to connection. In fact, if we notice that we've made a judgment, we could choose to find out what's behind the judgment in order to learn from the experience—to acknowledge the feelings and needs of our heart. A personal inventory of this type is called self-empathy in NVC and will be covered in more detail later.

We can put acceptance into action by observing the outside world without judging it; this helps us see the world more closely. We judge when we add our own subjectivity, analysis or labels to what we experience. Observations free us from our own subjectivity and allow us to make value judgments to determine whether needs are being met.

Differentiating between observations and evaluations is essential for communicating compassionately. Evaluation, especially in the form of criticism, often severs our connection. When describing an experience to others, observation may strengthen connection, especially when offered with caring and an intention of love.

Our ability to learn from life experiences is enhanced when we avoid judgments. We can choose to learn from life instead of judging ourselves as bad and feeling miserable. Learning from experience can prevent us from repeating the strategies that did not meet our needs.

The feeling of shame is associated with the message *I am bad*. Guilt is associated with *I have done something bad*. Instead of interpreting our actions as good or bad, we can use the terms *more effective* and *less effective* to describe whether an action helped us meet our needs. Self-empathy helps us to identify needs that are stimulated, and we can see if our strategies are working. If we want to connect, we make value judgments and let go of moral judgments.

Moral judgment doesn't foster growth or the love and connection we want. If I make a judgment, I acknowledge it with care and ask myself what's really going on. I give myself the empathy and grace that God gave me while searching out the feelings and needs behind my experience.

My experience is that communities centered on judgment have inhibited my ability to take responsibility for my actions and grow from them. Nonjudgmental groups and communities built around acceptance provide the greatest opportunity for growth.

Unsolicited advice, however well-intended, runs the risk of alienating the listener, who may want to work out things their own way. Their needs for choice, autonomy, and connection may not be met, making it more difficult for them to take in the message of the well-intended advice giver, as in this parable.

Do not give dogs what is sacred; do not throw your pearls to pigs. If you do, they may trample them under their feet, and then turn and tear you to pieces. (Matthew 7:6, NIV)

The foundation of Christianity is loving God and other people as much as we love ourselves, with all our heart, mind, soul, and strength.[26] It is about a life journey toward reestablishing our loving connection to God, ourselves, and others by following the Way of Christ. It is about finding ways to love not only people who are nice to us, but our enemies as well. As we saw in the Garden story, judgments of ourselves and others keep us from connecting with each other and from connecting with God.

13.

What's Behind Judgment?

Every judgment is a tragic expression of an unmet need. – Marshall Rosenberg

What's behind judgment, and why is it so prevalent? Here is a list of the most common needs behind judgment. Tragically, many are often met at the expense of another person's needs and our other needs, which can break a connection.[27]

- *Contribution.* The intention behind a judgment may be to contribute to someone's learning. The disconnection happens often because the listener may not want the feedback, and may become annoyed at getting the judgment because their needs for understanding, empathy, and autonomy are not met. The recipient doesn't want the gift being offered.

- *Safety.* Labeling someone or something as good, bad, or evil may meet one's need for safety. Putting such a label on something that is complex or experienced with fear, anxiety, and anger brings about some relief. Some people prefer judgment because it puts them in a superior position, making them feel safer.

- *Acceptance.* People might choose to deny their true humanness, to reject the notion that they have needs like every other being, due to a fear of rejection. They think that if they take the offensive and judge, they are somehow immune to judgment. Deep inside, however, they long for acceptance.

- *Freedom, Autonomy.* As we judge, we might tell ourselves that we sit in the seat of Moses, as if we are not subject to the law and can do whatever we please. Judgment also makes us feel stronger, invulnerable, need-less, as if we can operate independently of God and others. Judgment is especially helpful if we don't believe there are any caring people who will be there for us in our hour of need.

- *Empowerment.* We judge because it gives us the illusion of power over others. Our neediness is too dangerous to accept, so we take the action of judgment and shift responsibility for our feelings and needs to others, becoming *victims*[28] to them.

- *Clarity.* Putting labels on concepts or situations that may be complicated, unfamiliar, or painful can bring a sense of clarity. We believe that the situation at hand is now understood because a label has been put on it. Labeling gives the illusion of understanding.

- *Belonging.* When groups of people come together with a common set of tightly held beliefs that include the judgment of others, a sense of belonging can be created. Problems may arise when members question some of the beliefs of the group based on their own needs for clarity, freedom, understanding, integrity, and autonomy.

- *Justice, Fairness.* If we tell ourselves that someone is not playing fair or following our agreements, we often believe that we know better and we want to tell the other person that they did it wrong. We want to punish them.

- *Support.* Because needs are temporarily met by judgment, groups of people can be used to support the needs of those in charge of the group.[29] They miss the mark when they meet some needs at the expense of participants' other needs.

Those who judge are often more critical of themselves than they are of those who have grace and are therefore shown mercy. Letting go of judgment takes knowledge of a loving Creator and faith that there's a multitude of ways to get needs met because God created an abundant universe. A relationship with God, which is fostered by time alone in prayer, supports the connection that allows our needs to be met in ways that the Holy Spirit can help us to discover. This relationship with God also supports our developing the courage to engage other human beings in a dialogue of the heart, exploring ways we can get our needs met. All in all, judgment feels less risky and less vulnerable than admitting that we have needs. Only those who are willing to step out in faith and learn the joy of interdependence can escape the tyranny of judgment.

Because of the power of judgment and its implications for people who hold positions of power, the concepts and interpretations in this book may be strongly opposed. Judgment is a strategy used by many in positions of authority to maintain their power, to the detriment of those who follow them. In NVC, this is called a *power-over position* in a hierarchy.

Being blind and unaware is the metaphorical meaning behind the serpent as it remains hidden in its goal to deceive people into eating from the Tree of Judgment.[30]

14.

Needs Are Often Confused with Strategies

I do not give to you the way the world gives. (John 14:27, NIV)

We have discussed needs but have not yet discussed strategies. A strategy in the context of NVC is an action taken in order to meet a need. Strategies are focused on specific people, places, or things, whereas needs are independent of them. For example, saying *I need a cup of coffee in the morning* — is a statement that, when translated by NVC, coffee is identified as a strategy that meets my needs for aliveness and comfort in the morning.

Saying *I need a cheeseburger* is really a strategy for meeting my needs for nourishment and perhaps comfort. One way to tell the difference between a need and a strategy is that needs are universal; everyone has them. But strategies are individual; not everyone employs the same strategies to meet the same need. We all have needs for aliveness, nourishment, and comfort that are stimulated at one time or another. However, not everyone drinks coffee or eats cheeseburgers — these are strategies.

If I depend on a specific strategy to meet a need, this is sometimes described as living in scarcity. If I use only coffee to meet my needs for aliveness and comfort in the morning, I'll have a huge problem if coffee is not available. If the coffee runs out and the weather is nice outside, I could choose to go jogging to meet my needs. If it's raining31 and I don't feel like getting wet, I could jog on the treadmill, do yoga, or exercise indoors.

There is an infinite number of strategies available to us to satisfy our needs. The whole of God's creation is available to help us find strategies that work for ourselves and others. It's much easier for us to find mutually agreeable solutions from this heart-connected place, as God will help us meet our needs.

Once our needs are clear and we are connected to them, we may choose a strategy that invites a specific person, place, thing, or action to meet a need. This is our attempt at meeting a need to the best of our ability. Sometimes our strategies work, sometimes they don't; sometimes they work in some ways but not in others. Any time I feel that something is not in harmony with my heart, I can choose to return to my needs to get clear on what's alive in the moment.

There are times when letting go of the strategy is difficult. For example, there was a time in my life when I thought my wife had to meet all my needs, and she had a similar belief. Our marriage didn't last long after one of us woke up and saw a need for community that the other person did not have. I used to smoke cigarettes whenever I felt anxiety; smoking was my strategy to deal with my feelings. Once it became clear to me that smoking was affecting my health to the point of giving me bronchitis and smoker's cough, I chose to quit smoking and exercise more—and I learned a language of the heart from NVC to express my feelings.

In recovery circles, it is said that letting go leads to freedom. In NVC language, when you let go of the strategy and connect with the needs, you will find freedom in the abundance of possibilities. When you choose to focus on the underlying needs, you come closer to discovering the truth behind your experiences.

Most conflict and addiction develops as a result of confusing needs and strategies. Staying connected to your needs and striving to understand the needs of others facilitates understanding, connection, and love. Given that different people have their own unique experience, it becomes imperative that we learn a language that facilitates a dialogue about our needs so that we can get clear with them and then help another to get clear with theirs. Without this distinction, it is likely that disagreement or conflict will arise. It helps if each person is willing to look inside through self-empathy before looking to others to get their needs met.

In short, we can differ on strategies, but we all share the same needs, which are in perfect harmony because they come from God. Strategies are earthly, human-made choices. Returning to the heart of God within us brings an abundance of options and endless possibilities.

15.

Rejecting the Gift?

I remember this event as if it were yesterday. I must have been four years old, because I remember my sister being a baby. Our family was in Kansas City to celebrate Christmas at our grandparents' house. I was excited about opening presents. The funny thing is, I only remember one — the gift I rejected.

My grandmother Bonnie's friend and neighbor from across the street, Mrs. Davis, had come over to celebrate Christmas with us. I remember being surprised that she had made the effort to get me something, since I really didn't know her. I sat on the floor facing the Christmas tree and unwrapped the red and white paper around the first gift: a book titled *Raggedy Andy Stories*.[32]

I said, "I don't want this!"

There was a silence in the room for a few moments. I'm guessing my mother was feeling sad around her need for harmony not being met; but seizing the moment, she asked me to follow her upstairs. She held my hand as we walked up the stairs toward Grandma's room. I remember taking those steps as if in a movie played in slow motion. I was curious and maybe a little concerned, as I hadn't learned what it meant to be in trouble yet. I distinctly remember her brief message, which she delivered in what I experienced as a soft, kind, and gentle manner. Her words went something like this.

Mrs. Davis is a friend of ours. She gave you this gift out of love in the spirit of Christmas. I know this is something you may not want, but it would be nice to tell her thank you and take the gift anyway.

After hearing my mother's words, I remember feeling something I now call regret. We walked down the stairs together, holding hands again. I went over to Mrs. Davis, gave her a hug, and said, "Thank you."

In the moment leading up to the hug, I remember wondering if she still liked me and if she was going to treat me any differently. She said something soothing, but her words escape me. I remember her smile and the feeling of warmth and caring I felt afterward.

I often think of this story when thinking of God's love for me and everything that he has created and given to me. I am especially moved when I ponder those things he placed in my heart.

Which of you, if his son asks for bread, will give him a stone? Or if he asks for a fish, will give him a snake? If you, then, though you are evil, know how to give good gifts to your children, how much more will your Father in heaven give good gifts to those who ask him! So in everything, do to others what you would have them do to you, for this sums up the Law and the Prophets. (Matthew 7:9-12, NIV)

Needs are a gift from God, and it doesn't make sense to reject them. Feelings and needs are like an internal compass helping us discern what life is saying to us in the moment. Needs are a constant reminder to move toward being true to our hearts, which bear the image of God.

Given the difference between needs and strategies, it's important to value our needs and let go of our strategies for getting them met. As we connect to the beauty of our needs, we discover an abundance of possible strategies to choose from while staying in harmony with our needs and those of others.

We can make requests of others, let go of the outcome, and know that we can choose to return to the abundance of needs. We rest in knowing that our creator, God, loves us and will support our life journey, and that we can share our journey with others. We are not alone.

Occasionally, we may get some of our needs met at the expense of other needs. Other times we may get our needs met at the expense of other people's needs, and sometimes we may meet other people's needs at the expense of our own. The next chapter discusses the dynamics of missing the mark related to the gift of needs, and the meaning of sin in light of this new understanding.

16.

Sin as Missing the Mark

The law is written on their hearts. (Romans 2:15, NIV)

One definition of sin is *to miss the mark*. In the Hebrew Bible, the generic word for sin is *het*, meaning "to err, to miss the mark." It does not mean "to do evil." The Greek word *hamartia* (ἁμαρτία) is usually translated as *sin* in the New Testament. In classical Greek, it means *to miss the mark* or *to miss the target*. The word was also used in Old English to describe archery.[33]

Thomas Bokenkotter writes:

> There are four different Hebrew root words that can be translated as *sin*. They convey differing nuances of meaning, such as to violate a legal norm, to go astray, to rebel, to err. But the Hebrews used many other words to convey the meaning of sin, including disorder, foolishness, guilt. But however they described it, sin for Israel was always rupture of their relationship to God.[34]

These definitions of sin are consistent with needs language in NVC. When we sin, we are missing something in our hearts that longs for harmony within itself; this also pulls us away from the expression of life to its fullest.[35] The mark represents our needs, which are a constant reminder of the love of God for us and within us.

Needs are represented by words that describe the things we need, value, and consider an integral part of who we are. Needs are a gift from God through which he gives us life. Needs contain information from God on how we are to live. This is consistent with Richard Rohr's definition of sin as a state of alienation or separateness caused by needs not met.[36]

Determining our needs and the needs of others helps us to live in harmony with God's love and to love each other. Sin with regard to needs can be seen as having three aspects.

- *Getting my needs met at the expense of other people's needs.* Traditionally, this has been called a selfish way of being. I might use my title or position to control the agenda of a meeting, knowing that others have things they want to talk about; thus, I meet my need for contribution at the expense of others' need to be heard. One of my favorite examples is my strong desire to give unsolicited and unwanted advice to others, meeting my need for contribution at the expense of their autonomy, respect and consideration.

- *Meeting others' needs at the expense of my own.* This is sometimes called codependence. On the surface it may look like helping, but in reality my actions are not meeting all needs. For example, we might give money to support building houses in another country when we needed that money to buy food—we meet our need to contribute to another at the expense of our need for nourishment.

- *Meeting a need of mine at the expense of my other needs.* Sometimes the choices I make meet some needs while not meeting others. For example, I might eat a pound of chocolate, meeting my need for comfort at the expense of my long-term health. I might go out to a bar and get drunk with friends, meeting my needs for connection, freedom from anxiety, and fun, at the expense of my health. This is especially tragic when we are dependent on a strategy, like gambling or drinking alcohol, that consumes resources that are needed to support our families—we are meeting needs for comfort and peace at the expense of our contribution to the many needs of our family (food, shelter, education, connection, etc.).

When we sin, we lose connection with God, ourselves, and other people. Sin is the act of missing the heart of love. NVC helps us to participate in a dialogue about our needs. Given this definition of sin, we have more clarity regarding what it means to live not only valuing others, but also valuing our relationship with God and valuing our own existence as a gift. We understand more fully that we are humans bearing the image of God.

This leads to the empowering understanding that we are the only ones who can know what we feel and what we need in the moment. By having this conversation with ourselves and God, we clearly define the lines of responsibility, facilitating a dialogue with others about strategies that consider everyone's needs. This is much more productive than judging others or beating up on ourselves.

As children, our parents had to guess at our needs before we could talk. Some of us continue to wish that others know our needs without our having to verbalize them; this wish destroys intimate relationships when it continues without being checked. As an adult, you'll find it helpful and empowering to develop an awareness of your needs and to gain the tools to express them with others in a way that respects them.

If our relationship with God as told in Genesis 1-3 had been the end of the story, we could have remained distant, fearful, and guarded from the Tree of Life. I imagine that even as Adam and Eve left the Garden, God had a plan to restore a loving connection with us. He sent Jesus to deliver the message and show us a path back to the Garden, the way to the Tree of Life that would restore harmony, intimacy, and communion with him.

Living in the spirit of Jesus's message leads to eternal life that is available to us now. If we are open and willing to engage each other through grace and truth in conversation, we may find the path that leads to life. His spirit takes care of the details. Jesus's *Way* and the message of how we may follow him through conversation is the subject of the next section.

III.

SERMON OF THE MASTER

Imagine that your favorite and beloved poet, who has been retired for thirty years, decides to invite a few friends over to share her latest works. She doesn't travel far because of her advanced age. She lives in a cluster of hills in an otherwise flat desert. You've been concerned for some time that she won't be with us much longer and are excited to hear that she is opening this gathering to her close friends and their friends.

Word of the event travels quickly through a grapevine of intimacy. The poet perches herself on her favorite boulder on the side of a hill and begins to talk about the life she's led since she went into seclusion. More and more people arrive. When the poet pauses to take a drink, it's so quiet that the only sounds are the wind blowing through the hills and the steps of the new arrivals crunching on the gravel.

The beloved poet recalls the sources of her poems one after another, and you're amazed at the wisdom in her words. You begin to feel warm and tingly inside; things become clearer as you listen. You are drawn to lean forward and move closer as the wind whispers louder. You lose track of time and realize you didn't bring enough food for the day. Then the person next to you hands you a basket filled with colorful foods. You take what you need and pass it on.

As the sun begins to set, the poet retires for the evening in deep gratitude for her chance to be heard, to be known, and to contribute to the well-being of others. She invites everyone to stay for breakfast the next morning, as she plans to personally connect with her friends.

As night falls upon the hill, a full moon provides enough light to cast a shadow. Drumming, dancing, and singing break out around the rocky fire pits.

This is how I imagine the Sermon on the Mount. In the middle of a desolate, rocky land, Jesus spoke, and his words brought clarity and hope to those who hungered for freedom, acceptance, and love.

In this section, I explore how Jesus's sermon invites us into greater intimacy with God and each other by developing an awareness of the elements of communication and how NVC helps us put them into practice.

The kingdom of heaven is like treasure hidden in a field. When a man found it, he hid it again, and then in his joy went and sold all he had and bought that field. Again, the kingdom of heaven is like a merchant looking for fine pearls. When he found one of great value, he went away and sold everything he had and bought it. (Matthew 13:44–46, NIV)

I've been on a treasure hunt for many years. There's something inside me that hungers for life to its fullest and wants my heart's desires fulfilled. I want eternal life in blissful connection to God and to others. Do you?

What comes up for you as you read this paragraph? Can you be honest enough to put it into words? Here's what I was thinking for a while. *Who am I to want all this life stuff? I'm not worthy. I'll never get it right, I'll never find it. It's too complicated.* And then I started to wonder, *Why is it hidden? Why is there so much suffering in the world? Why is there so much poverty and inequity? If God loves us so much, why does he hide the treasure?*

The story of Adam and Eve continues to be played out today. God gave us free will and the power to exercise it at every moment of our lives. The Tree of Judgment is always nearby, and it keeps us from the treasure as we continue to eat from it.

Jesus is trying to help us find our way back to the treasure. He tells us in different ways because we have difficulty understanding the message. He tells us to follow his teachings and the truth of the Kingdom will be revealed to us. The answer to the riddle is not a destination, but a path of love. As we walk this path in relationships, the Holy Spirit reveals the treasure to us.

Grace and Truth came through Jesus Christ. (John 1:17, NIV)

Jesus came to restore our intimate connection to God by showing us a path through grace and truth. As we are connected in our hearts, we hear the voice of God speaking to us, inviting us to love ourselves as his wonderful creations and to love each other in the same way.

Whoever drinks the water I give him will never thirst. Indeed, the water I give him will become a spring of water welling up to eternal life. (John 4:14, NIV)

By following Jesus's teachings, we can transform our life to transcend our human suffering. We find our one true source of life, which then becomes our own fountain providing spiritual water that sustains life. We feel his grace envelop our being, enabling us to extend it to others.

In him was life and that life was the light of men. (John 1:4, NIV)

Jesus spoke to us in hope that we would hear and understand his message. Through his words, we ask, seek, and knock, and eventually the truth about ourselves is revealed to us. The veil is lifted and we feel God, even if only for an instant. As we live in connection with God, and in harmony within the heart made in his image, the radiant light of who we are shines brightly for all to see. The light and water contribute to nurturing the fruit of the vine connected to the Tree of Life so that as we eat from this tree, we discover and celebrate the reason we live in this world.

Discussion

- Were you able to relate to the story of the beloved poet?
- How do you imagine Jesus's surroundings when he was giving the Sermon on the Mount?
- What do *grace* and *truth* mean to you? How do they appear in your daily life?
- What do the metaphors of water and light mean to you?

17.

The Be-Attitudes

In the beginning of the Sermon on the Mount, as told in Matthew 5:3–11 (NLT), Jesus gives us clues on how to get to the Kingdom. These are not demands, but an invitation into the heart. Jesus used the word *blessed* nine times, at the beginning of each of his exhortations. The definition of *blessed* is to celebrate with praises[37] and to make or pronounce as holy; to consecrate.[38] The main point Jesus was trying to make is that what follows *blessed* points us in the direction of the Kingdom. The words are markers on a path. If we want to find the treasure, then we certainly want to investigate these clues and bring them along on our journey.

You may have read these verses hundreds of times and heard many interpretations. I invite you to hear these words anew and to hear the heart within you.

God blesses those who are poor and realize their need for him, for the Kingdom of Heaven is theirs.

Jesus started the Sermon by highlighting our need for God; this is an encouragement to let go of our ego identifications in favor of humbly owning our needs as given to us by God from the very beginning. God created us with a need to love him and other people.

God's love for us is expressed through the needs and values of our hearts. Jesus begins with a list of important heart needs; my associated heart words are noted in parentheses below. Read the verses slowly; soak in the beauty that Jesus is inviting you to consider. Take time between verses. Let them speak to you, and consider the needs in his message.

God blesses those who mourn,
for they will be comforted.

(Healing, Comfort)

God blesses those who are humble,
for they will inherit the whole earth.

(Hope, Equality)

God blesses those who hunger and thirst for justice,
for they will be satisfied.

(Justice)

God blesses those who are merciful,
for they will be shown mercy.

(Compassion, Understanding)

God blesses those whose hearts are pure,
for they will see God.

(Honesty, Empathy, Communion)

God blesses those who work for peace,
for they will be called the children of God.

(Peace, Harmony, Mutuality,
Belonging, Community)

God blesses those who are persecuted for doing right,
for the Kingdom of Heaven is theirs.

(Service, Justice, Contribution)

By listening with our hearts, we are able to hear and feel the life current behind the written words. For example, in Matthew 5: 13–17, I hear this.

You who are my disciples are to demonstrate my teaching through your life, by the way in which you live. By being yourselves, you bring passion and enjoyment to life as salt brings flavor to a meal.

As you live in the spirit, you bring encouragement and hope to those who listen. You contribute clarity of purpose that only love can show. You are like a light to the world, helping people see in places that used to be dark.

As I have told you before, I have not come to destroy the law, but to bring meaning and fulfillment to it. I come to build the Kingdom, not to destroy the world.

My invitation is to live in integrity, where the voice of your heart matches the actions you take.

Always take responsibility for your experience, and strive for harmony and peace with everyone, especially those with whom you have conflict. Listen to their hearts and be willing to share yours. The Holy Spirit will help you to find solutions to meet your needs.

Honor your agreements with others, and be fair with those who have less power than you do. Consider their needs to be as important as yours. Show respect to all, especially to God. Please don't use the name of God lightly or blame God when things don't work out the way you want them to. There may be a lesson for you to learn instead.

Strive for integrity and honesty so that when you say yes, you really mean it and will follow through on your agreement. At the same time, if you cannot fulfill someone's request with joy, saying no is appropriate. If your no is consistent with your heart, say it!

In the next set of verses, Jesus lists some real-life situations that his audience might have encountered in their day. I am grateful to Walter Wink for pointing out the significance of these verses.[39]

You have heard that it was said, Eye for eye, and tooth for tooth. *But I tell you, do not resist an evil person. If someone strikes you on the right cheek, turn to him the other also.*

If someone wants to sue you and take your tunic, let him have your cloak as well.

If someone forces you to go one mile, go with him two miles.
(Matthew 5:39–43, NIV)

These verses are filled with creative ways that a person of little means and no power can express their needs in difficult situations. If someone struck me on the right cheek, it was a result of a backhand from a right-handed person, which in ancient times was a sign of humiliation used to put servants in their place. At the time of Jesus, there existed great inequality between rich and poor, and often people with power and wealth had servants to attend to their needs. For a servant to retaliate from a backhand with force would be suicide. But turning the other cheek is an invitation to be treated as an equal, to be struck with the forehand, addressing the servant's needs for mutual respect while at the same time following the law of servitude for their master.

On the issue of being sued, in times of great inequality between rich and poor, if everything you own is being demanded, then to surrender your cloak as well as your tunic would leave you naked in the court. In those days, humiliation fell to the person viewing a naked person, not to the person exposed. Community shame fell upon the person suing because everyone would hear about the injustice of taking everything from someone who had so little to give.

In Roman times, a soldier could ask anyone to help him carry his gear for a mile. To refuse to act as ordered was dangerous, given the Roman superiority in power and position. I imagine that the man carrying the gear struck up a conversation with the soldier, and during the first mile, they developed a sense of connection. Then, as they crossed the mile mark, the conversation continued, and the many carrying the gear insisted on continuing to carry the soldier's gear. But think of the humor in the person carrying the gear and continuing to carry it, trying to be a grateful servant—even as the Roman soldier asks for the gear back, wanting to show respect to his new friendship and also having concern for the rules. The rule limiting the soldier was to have the person carry the gear for no more than a mile, or risk trouble with his commanding officer.

In these verses, Jesus invites us to consider new and creative ways to respond to injustice. In fact, Jesus is saying that we do not have to give in to our natural urges toward fight, flight, or freeze, but that we can stand in strength and face our enemies in this new light, inviting the oppressor to consider a higher truth by our actions and words. Jesus abhors passivity and violence as responses to evil and invites us to find creative ways in which the humanity of all parties is restored[40] when everyone's needs are considered.

In short, Jesus invites us to consider new ways to deal with conflict. He rejects the outward use of violence as he invites us to be open to solutions that consider the needs of everyone involved. Having an awareness of our internal conversation is essential to living in harmony with the gospel message of loving our neighbors and even our enemies as well as ourselves.

Discussion

- What heart needs did you hear Jesus express in the Beatitudes? Are you in agreement with the ones listed by the author?
- Which verse was your favorite and why?
- Do you agree with the stated significance of the "right cheek" in Matthew 5:39? If not, how would you interpret it?
- Do you see any significance in going one mile versus two miles?

18.

Loving God, Self, Others

"Teacher, which is the greatest commandment in the Law?" Jesus replied, "Love the Lord your God with all your heart and with all your soul and with all your mind. This is the first and greatest commandment. And the second is like it: 'Love your neighbor as yourself.' All the Law and the Prophets hang on these two commandments." (Matthew 22:36–40, NIV)

I am inspired when I read the message of love so central to Jesus's teachings. I have always believed it to be true, though I have not always experienced it. Jesus tells us to love not only God, but others as well as ourselves. This brings out the question, *What is love?*

The meaning of love seems to be different for everyone. Some experience love when they receive a gift, others when they are acknowledged, when they are touched or hugged, when they spend quality time together, or when they serve or are served.[41] Gary Chapman's research suggests that people define and experience love differently. There are numerous interpretations of the meaning of love, and I've chosen some from *The Four Loves* by C.S. Lewis (and a few snippets from Wikipedia).[42]

Affection (storge, στοργή) is a fondness through familiarity, especially between family members or people who have come together by chance. It is described as the most natural, emotive, and widely diffused of loves: it is natural in that it is present without coercion; emotive because it is fondness due to familiarity; and most widely diffused because it pays little attention to characteristics deemed "valuable" or "worthy" of love and as a result is able to see past most factors used for judgment.

Friendship (*philia*, φιλία) is a bond existing between people who share a common interest or activity. Lewis states that his definition of friendship is narrower than mere companionship. Friendship in his sense only exists if there is something for the friendship to be "about." Friendship is the least natural of loves, says Lewis: it isn't biologically necessary to progeny, like Eros (creating a child), affection (rearing a child), or charity (providing for a child). Friendship has the least association with impulse or emotion.

Eros (ἔρως) is love in the sense of *being in love*. This is distinct from sexuality, which Lewis calls Venus, although he does spend time discussing sexual activity and its spiritual significance in both a pagan and Christian sense. He identifies Eros as openhanded, promoting appreciation of the beloved regardless of the pleasure received.

Charity (*agapē*, ἀγάπη) is the love that brings forth caring regardless of circumstance. Lewis recognizes this as the greatest of loves. Lewis says that the love of God "is so full that it overflows, and He can't help but love us." Lewis compares love with a garden, charity with the gardening utensils, the lover with a gardener, and God as the elements of nature. God's love and guidance act on our natural love as the sun and rain act on a garden: without either, the garden would cease to be beautiful or beneficent.

The Greek word used in the verses above is *agape*, meaning generally unconditional love or unconditional positive regard and acceptance—what Lewis calls charity. The closest thing to agape that I've experienced is being a parent to my son Alex. I sang and played guitar for him before he was born. I remember the excitement I felt at hearing his heartbeat for the first time. But our connection really intensified when I locked eyes with him the moment he was born, and something in me was changed forever. It was the most significant day of my life up to that point. As I gazed at him, it was as if he were saying, "Okay, Dad, I'm here. Now what?"

From that moment forward, some unexplainable force within me invites me to contribute to his well-being and brings me joy. And that desire has continued throughout my life and has deepened steadily as we both continue to grow. Perhaps the intensity of our connection is in part because he and I live apart most of the time. We do not take each other for granted. It's quite the opposite; the time we spend together is intense and filled with adventure and fun. When we're apart, I experience the sadness of not being there for him. What I want to do is contribute directly to his well-being and provide physical support through my presence, encouragement, and protection.

I have wondered about the bigger reasons why my son and I ended up living in different states, and what lesson there is in my life experience. My relationship and subsequent divorce from his mother provided rich soil to propel my growth. My gut tells me that God wanted me to experience, however small in comparison, what he might feel for us. This resonates as true for me and brings tears to my eyes. Being Alex's dad is the best thing that's ever happened to me. I could write a book on my relationship with him; perhaps someday I will.

My love for my son is closest to my understanding of agape, the kind of love that God has for us and invites us to share together. In agape we must recognize and value the heart, celebrating it as a gift from God. The more time we spend in celebration, the more gratitude and warmth we feel, compelling us to share this gift with others and invite them to share their hearts with one another through experiences, life stories, connection, play, dance, and sharing meals in our homes. The sharing occurs only if the other person is open to receive and accept the invitation; otherwise we'd be missing the mark.

By recalling these gifts of the heart, I am able to experience love in many ways beyond being a parent. I can experience love through beauty, through adventure, through my struggle for meaning, through giving and receiving support, through my desire for justice and mutual respect, through mutual understanding—through all that is in my heart. I experience love as I acknowledge all this as part of the Heart of God within us—things that call out my relationship with God as a being created in his image. When I celebrate the heart needs within my being, I experience the love of God as I experience love for others and for myself.

God is love. (1 John 4:8, 4:16, NIV)

For God so loved the world that he gave his one and only Son. (John 3:16, NIV)

The message of Jesus is a return to God, who is love. And all of the heart needs are different manifestations of God's desire that we experience love for everyone including ourselves, as each one of us is a precious created being. All the gifts of creation are an abundant reminder of the reason we are here in the first place: to experience love.

Discussion

- What is your meaning for the word love? How does this play out in your relationships?
- Did this chapter expand your understanding of love? If so, how?

- Why do you think God placed a need for love in our hearts?

- How does love serve God's plans for the world?

- How do you express love toward others? Give an example.

- How well is your expression of love received by those who hear it?

- Do you desire a deeper loving connection with others? What thoughts come up as you ponder this question?

19.

Who Is Your Neighbor?

The man wanted to justify himself, so he asked Jesus, "Who is my neighbor?" In reply, Jesus said

A man was going down from Jerusalem to Jericho when he fell into the hands of robbers. They stripped him of his clothes, beat him, and went away, leaving him half dead. A priest happened to be going down the same road, and when he saw the man, he passed by on the other side. So too, a Levite, when he came to the place and saw him, passed by on the other side.

But a Samaritan, as he traveled, came where the man was; and when he saw him, he took pity on him.[43] *He went to him and bandaged his wounds, pouring on oil and wine. Then he put the man on his own donkey, took him to an inn and took care of him. The next day he took out two silver coins and gave them to the innkeeper. "Look after him," he said, "And when I return, I will reimburse you for any extra expense you may have."*

Which of these three do you think was a neighbor to the man who fell into the hands of robbers?

The expert in the law replied, "The one who had mercy on him." Jesus told him, Go and do likewise. (Luke 10:29–37, NIV)

In the parable of the Good Samaritan, Jesus shows us that our neighbor is anyone willing to contribute to the needs of others who are open to receiving help. I searched translations of this parable for the word *good* but didn't find it in the text; the word *compassionate* more accurately describes the Samaritan, so I'll refer to this text as the parable of the Compassionate Samaritan.

A friend of mine told me that this parable was used extensively in her youth to guilt her into doing service and donating money. It was clear from our dialogue that she still had some pain around it. Her needs for autonomy, choice, and respect had not been met. My friend needed empathy for her pain.

As we acknowledge our feelings and needs, we find healing from our pain, resulting in feelings of compassion and curiosity about others. After receiving empathy, we see that other people's needs are as valuable as our own. We can contribute to others freely and meet our needs for autonomy, choice, and respect. We feel joy in serving others.

Jesus invites us to consider giving and receiving, not out of duty or obligation, not to buy someone's love, but to give with integrity. It's important that our external actions match the condition of our heart, for then we feel joy.

At the end of his journey, I'm guessing that the injured man was feeling deeply grateful, perhaps bordering on ecstatic, as his needs for support, caring, and health were met. He was humbly open to having his needs met. He was in a position to receive from anyone willing to offer assistance, and help would be welcome.

There's a message here: it's important to be humble, willing, honest, and open to one another with our needs. In order to live out this truth, it's vital to recognize it within ourselves first and then verbalize it to others. In NVC, this is called *honest expression.*

For the injured man in the parable, his needs were obvious to all who passed by. He might have been crying in pain, with tears rolling down his face, perhaps bleeding. He communicated his needs using his voice, his tears, and his blood.

Our injuries are not only physical, but also emotional. We might be feeling hurt, pain, sadness, despair, anxiety, or fear. I would be the injured person in the parable when I'm willing to reveal my feelings and needs to those who are willing to listen and empathize with me. I can also be the Compassionate Samaritan for another human being. When they are in need, I can choose to be a willing participant in God's master plan of love. With the simple act of being present, listening, helping them identify their needs, and being open to finding solutions that meet those needs, I am ultimately choosing to be the Compassionate Samaritan.

One distinction must be made clear, however. When I carry out acts of compassion for another human being, they must be in harmony with my own needs as well. If they are not, I am not being compassionate to myself.

You too can play the roles of the injured person and the Compassionate Samaritan. I've noticed that I feel more comfortable playing the role of the Samaritan than the role of the injured person. Going on mission trips to serve the "poor and needy" is easier. To admit the truth of my experience, that I'm also hurt, crying, and bleeding, is more difficult. Often I'm afraid my needs for consideration, respect, and safety will not be met if I am vulnerable, so I keep them to myself.

When I assumed the role of Compassionate Samaritan, I used to believe that my job was to fix someone's feelings; now I know it is not. I once believed that others expected me to take on their feelings; now I know that I have the power to choose how I listen to others. I don't have to take on someone else's feelings if I don't want to. At the same time, I allow myself to feel whatever comes up naturally as I listen. And I have learned how to express my feelings and needs to others if I so choose and if they are willing to listen.

In this same parable Jesus also taught that "our brother" could be anyone, even enemies like the Samaritans, who were hated by the Jews at that time. Geza Vermes says that "Samaritans were hated by the story's target audience, the Jews, to such a degree that the lawyer did not mention them by name but as *the one who had mercy on him.*"[44] The Samaritans in turn hated the Jews. The enmity was in essence religious: both groups accused each other of misinterpreting the Torah, of falsely considering themselves God's chosen people, and of conducting false worship, unacceptable to God.

Jesus made the point that God calls us to love everyone and to respect and value their needs as much as our own. He said that love goes beyond what we may feel comfortable with. Jesus confronted prejudice against people from other cultures and beliefs and broke tradition by speaking to women, which was taboo for a rabbi at that time, especially in public (see John 4:4–21).

In the parable of the Compassionate Samaritan, Jesus made the point that anyone in need is to be considered our neighbor and that the Samaritan's interaction with the injured man was a model for how agape can be experienced. Both roles are important in a conversation motivated by love.

Jesus also gives us other examples in which these roles are played out. He invites us to consider what children have to offer us, which we cover in the next chapter.

Discussion

- Have you ever experienced compassion from a stranger? Please share your story.
- Can you identify the judgments in the cultural dialogue between Jews and Samaritans? What do you think was the effect of those judgments?
- What culturally biased judgments exist in our society today?
- Do you find your actions and words supporting cultural biases? How?

20.

Being Like Little Children

At that time the disciples came to Jesus and asked, "Who is the greatest in the kingdom of heaven?" He called a little child and had him stand among them, and he said, I tell you the truth, unless you change and become like little children, you will never enter the kingdom of heaven. Therefore, whoever humbles himself like this child is the greatest in the kingdom of heaven. And whoever welcomes a little child like this in my name welcomes me. (Matthew 18:1–5, NIV)

It has been my experience that children have something innocent and pure about them that is essential to living a full life and is especially important in the type of conversations I describe in this book. I've observed many of these qualities in my son Alex, such as the following.

- He's open with his needs, now and when he was a baby and a toddler.
- He is honest.

- He openly celebrates everything he finds new and exciting.
- He openly mourns when his needs are not met.
- He asks for what he wants as best he can.
- He sleeps when he's tired.
- He wants his needs to be considered, to matter.
- He wants respect.
- He needs safety to go about exploring the world.

These examples can help us explore what Jesus meant when he said that becoming childlike is necessary for entering the Kingdom of Heaven. He was teaching about the attitude of our hearts and minds and about what is needed to eat from the Tree of Life. In a nutshell, our hearts and minds need to be open and present to the truth of our experience. They need to guide us so that we can show consideration and respect to others.

The injured person in the parable of the Compassionate Samaritan is like a child in that he

- Is honest and open with his needs.
- Openly mourns needs not met.
- Asked for what he wanted as best he could.
- Wants his needs to be considered.
- Wants to matter.
- Wants respect.

Jesus invites us to live with open hearts as a path toward the Kingdom of Heaven and to be vulnerable and truthful with others about our experience. He invites us into a deeper and more meaningful and fulfilling conversation. Children express themselves willingly and openly, even if the listener doesn't know how to respond. Jesus invites us to take risks with our honesty; as adults, finding safe places to express our honesty is important. Close friendships, twelve-step meetings, NVC practice groups, counseling sessions, interest groups, or support groups can offer safety and acceptance.

Other important qualities of a child are play and exploration. Watching children at play reminds me of Alex; it stirs my heart and brings me joy. Children enjoy their fresh experience of the world in many ways.

- They have a natural curiosity.
- They have an innocence that takes nothing for granted.
- They make few assumptions about the world, since most of it is new to them.
- They love to play.
- They love to be with others.

Sometimes a little play communicates more than intellectual analysis. Play helped me understand Jesus's message when Alex was thirteen and we went to the Texas Renaissance Festival. We were nearing the end of the day. Up to this point, we hadn't fenced with swords as we had done in the past, and he wasn't as playful as he used to be, possibly because the amusements weren't cool enough for him. Then we got to a tent that offered balancing balls on grooved wooden planks.[45] I could tell he was excited, because he left me without saying a word to play with the wooden balls.

I was surprised by his interest. This weekend, being a cool teenager seemed more important to him. I tried to balance the balls on my hands as the carny had demonstrated, but I was more interested in Alex than in balancing the balls. I walked a short distance to join a group listening to a Celtic band play. I kept an eye on Alex and enjoyed the music.

The drum's thunderous resonance made the ground vibrate as I listened to the talented musicians play "Amazing Grace."[46] With this as background, I was overwhelmed with joy at the beauty and simplicity of Alex's play, knowing that his openness to play in this fashion might diminish during his teenage years. Tears streamed down my face, and later I wrote this poem in honor of this memory.

My Playful Child

Innocent beauty of my playful child.
He plays without care as he balances a ball on the back of his hand.
I smile as he drops the ball, and quickly picks it up again.

He seems to be captured by the joy of his play.
Other children play around him equally enchanted.
Smiles and laughter are visible and heard.
They now decide to balance on wood.

They roll the ball from one board to another,
As each person moves the sphere to the right
Its balance that's needed, and care but not might.

After completing their handoff, they move even faster
If careless they are, it ends in disaster
Then each child goes to the end of the line
Each one of them goes, cycling through time.

I'm torn between the stillness of joy, and my desire to capture it.
Remember it I must, it's as pure as it gets.
I'm sad his teenage years advance, but joy that not quite yet.

I'm hopeful he'll keep some of his innocent play,
As I search in my heart for my own every day.

I want to return to the green rolling hill,
Beyond what is judgment and proving my skill.
To play and to be in the Garden again.
I hope I will see you there yonder, my friend.[47]

Discussion

- Can you identify with the qualities of the child and those of the injured man? Which ones, and how? If you don't identify with childlike qualities, why do you think that is?

- What thoughts occur to you when you think about being open with your feelings and needs as a little child?

- What are your feelings as you read the list of qualities of a child?

- What qualities of children do you enjoy the most?

- What do you think was Jesus's main point in the parable in Matthew 18:1-5?

- How can you become more childlike? What interferes with your becoming more childlike?

21.

Empathy as Grace

Grace can be defined as unmerited favor from God; it is the outpouring of the love of God for humanity. In the story of Adam and Eve in the Garden of Eden, our connection to God was lost when they ate from the Tree of Judgment. Through this act we assumed the role of judge, which we were not intended to have.

> *For God so loved the world that he gave his one and only Son, that whoever believes in him shall not perish but have eternal life. For God did not send his Son into the world to condemn the world, but to save the world through him.* (John 3:16–17, NIV)

Jesus came to extend grace to all of humanity by offering his message and teachings of love. Grace is related to the need for acceptance; God accepts anyone who accepts his love into their hearts. We were created as *very good.*[48]

I am amazed at the divisions caused by the concept of grace. Scholars spend a lot of time defining who goes to heaven and who doesn't, playing a role they were not intended to play. Instead of focusing my attention on things I cannot control, I choose to focus on putting into practice the teachings of Jesus through the character of the conversations I have with others. I strive to live in harmony with his message of love for God, other people, and myself. When it comes to the finer points of who gets to heaven, I leave that to God.

Grace is an important element of agape. Because of free will, in order to fully accept God's grace I must extend grace to myself first. As I receive God's grace, I begin to extend his grace to others through love by acting in concert with my heart needs.

For a period when I was young, I didn't extend grace to myself; I experienced dark times as a result. When I was a teenager and moved from Puerto Rico to Kansas, I felt like I didn't fit in. I told myself things like

I'm no good.
I'm different from them, and they're better than I am.
I'm poor and everybody else has plenty of money.

I believed the voices in my head, and they skewed my perception of reality. The following event reinforced the message.

We had just moved into my grandparents' home in Merriam while my parents looked for work and a place to live. My dad was working in the house and the garage, clearing out clutter, and he asked me if I'd help him. We drove our station wagon to a nearby dumpster behind a restaurant. As we started unloading the car, a man approached us, shouting, "Get out of here! You can't do that. This is our dumpster. Leave or I'm calling the cops!"

I was confused and a little fearful. Dad was stammering, "You don't have to talk to me that way ..."

The man kept shouting; it was clear that he didn't want a dialogue. The negative messages in my mind got louder and louder, reinforcing my feelings of shame. I'm sure my father was equally perplexed, and in his own way he was asking to be treated with respect and dignity. At the time, it seemed strange to me that anyone would care if we threw our trash in their dumpster. (I now know there is a cost for waste disposal and usually laws against dumping).

Dad and I got in the car and drove away. We were both silent all the way back to Grandma's house. I was processing the event, but I didn't feel comfortable talking about it to my dad. I was overwhelmed, confused, and embarrassed. My response to what had happened was to think, *I don't know the rules. I'm less than. I don't belong.*

I regret never talking to Dad about this event, and he has since died. I wish I knew how he experienced what happened that day.

I now see that I needed clarity from my dad to understand what was happening; I also needed safety and comfort before I could talk about it. I wish I had had the skills I have now; I would have offered my dad empathy, perhaps saying, "Dad, are you surprised by that man's words? Do you want more respect and consideration—to hear that your needs matter as much as theirs?" or "Dad, I'm guessing you would have liked more support and understanding."

The needs expressed in my empathy are the same ones that were alive for me. I judged the situation. But my judgment turned inward on myself, not toward the man who was yelling at us. The negative messages of my self-judgment blinded me to the truth. Metaphorically, I ate from the Tree of Judgment and judged myself to be less than.

Jesus shows us a different way. He tells us to let go of our judgments and to accept where we are. He invites us to listen to what we're telling ourselves about our experiences. He wants us to see what is really happening around us and within us.

Jesus came to offer us a gift of grace and to teach us ways to find freedom from the fruit of the Tree of Judgment and connect to the heart and mind of God.

> Do not judge, or you too will be judged. For in the same way you judge others, you will be judged, and with the measure you use, it will be measured to you.

> Why do you look at the speck of sawdust in your brother's eye and pay no attention to the plank in your own eye? How can you say to your brother, Let me take the speck out of your eye, when all the time there is a plank in your own eye? You hypocrite, first take the plank out of your own eye, and then you will see clearly to remove the speck from your brother's eye. (Matthew 7:1–5, NIV)

In the words "do not judge," Jesus reminds us to let go of the role of judge and instead look inside ourselves at the plank in our eye. My interpretation of the plank is everything that goes on within us. Taking the plank out of your eye is a metaphor for becoming aware of our internal dialogue. Jesus tells us to listen to and question our judgments, interpretations, experiences, motivations, and actions in order to learn and understand. When we remove the plank, we are able to see more clearly what's really going on.

This action of separating our inner conversation from what is really happening helps us to see the truth of our own experience, which then enables us help others so that they too can see their experiences more clearly.

The plank in my eye is much larger than the speck in my brother's eye. This is a clear indication that our inner judgments must be taken care of first because they can blind us to the truth. After I remove my plank, I'm better able to help remove the speck from my brother's eye, a metaphor for helping my brother become aware of his internal dialogue.

This discussion invites us to look inside. The following verses tell us what to do once we're there.

> *Keep on asking and you will receive what you ask for. Keep on seeking, and you will find. Keep on knocking, and the door will be opened to you, for everyone who asks, receives. Everyone who seeks, finds. And to everyone who knocks, the door will be opened.*

> *Parents, if your children ask for a loaf of bread, do you give them a stone instead? Or if they ask for a fish, do you give them a snake? Of course not. So if you sinful people know how to give good gifts to your children, how much more will your heavenly Father give good gifts to those who ask him.* (Matthew 7:7–11, NLT)

Jesus invites us to ask, seek, and knock to remove the plank. This dialogue starts with ourselves and then proceeds to others. If we do this with a heart of a child,[49] we will find what we seek, receive the clarity we ask for, and release the plank that weighs us down, blinding us to the truth of our experiences and keeping us from love. As we acknowledge the state of our hearts, we open the door to the Holy Spirit to work in our lives, allowing us to receive the abundance of "good gifts to those who ask."

Discussion

- Were you moved by this chapter? How did you feel about what moved you?
- What is your understanding of judgment and its effects in your life?
- What is your understanding of the metaphor of the plank and the speck?
- What are your ideas about how to go about removing the plank?

Self-Empathy

Be on your guard against the yeast of the Pharisees, which is hypocrisy. There is nothing concealed that will not be disclosed, or hidden that will not be made known. (Luke 12:1-3, NIV)

The process of removing our plank is called *self-empathy* in NVC. Hypocrisy is the act of persistently pretending to hold beliefs, opinions, virtues, feelings, qualities, or standards that one does not actually hold. In other words, our outward actions are not consistent with internal beliefs and the state of the heart. Self-empathy helps us clarify the truth of our experience and helps us live in integrity. As the opposite of hypocrisy, integrity directs us to act in harmony with the heart—when the inside is like the outside. When we are in integrity, we achieve a kind of self-similarity.[50]

Self-empathy is the most important process in NVC, for it is difficult to connect with and love others without it. It is a way of accepting God's grace, loving ourselves and honoring our own truths. It follows the same process we discussed earlier when we looked at the teachings of Jesus in the Gospel of Matthew. Once we acknowledge the heart, which was hidden by the plank, we open the door to the Holy Spirit to provide for our needs, either directly or by helping us find new strategies.

In NVC, the main elements of self-empathy are my observations, feelings, needs, and requests (OFNRs). For example, I might notice that my breathing has become shallow (observation). I'll ask myself, *What am I feeling?* and try to answer to the best of my ability. I may not be totally clear at that point, because sometimes it's difficult to know one's feelings right away, but I take a guess.

I'm feeling anxious.
I wonder what my needs are in the moment?
I'm guessing that I need safety.
What am I asking of myself?
Would I be willing to remove myself from this situation?

I could then choose to walk away and go through the self-empathy process a few more times until I get the clarity and understanding I want.

I grew up with the belief that being needy was a bad thing. In fact, I was encouraged to be selfless in giving—to give even when it hurt. It took me several years in recovery from what is called *codependence* to learn that this type of giving has a hidden dark side. I now see codependence as meeting the needs of others at the expense of my own. Without clearly identifying the needs I was trying to meet by my actions, I ended up sacrificing those and other needs in the process.

It's important to get clear with my own needs in the moment before I can consider someone else's needs and experiences. This was a difficult lesson to learn because I was so used to focusing my attention on others. I found that most of my childhood learning centered on looking outside myself for the cause of my discomfort. It took the form of blaming others, which is a direct result of eating from the Tree of Judgment.

My blaming others was hidden to me. I wasn't aware of my responsibility for my own experience. Listening to my feelings and taking responsibility for my needs was a vital and transforming step on my journey.

It is essential to our freedom to acknowledge the truth of our experiences and to honor what God is telling us at the moment it happens. One way God speaks to us is through our experiences, expressed in feelings and needs in our hearts. When we listen to our feelings and needs first, we can reframe our perception of needs as something that comes directly from God.

Needs are a beautiful gift from a loving God. They are the words that describe how love is manifested and expressed within us. We begin to feel more connected and healthier as we acknowledge the truth of our life experience, feeling joy and contentment as we swim in the experience of heart needs. We might ask ourselves questions about what to do to get our needs met and come up with several possibilities.

I feel tired, I recognize that I need rest, and I take steps to relax for a while. *Would I be willing to lie down for a twenty-minute afternoon nap?*

I notice my stomach is making sounds, and I'm feeling hungry—I need food. *Would I be willing to stop what I'm doing, take a thirty-minute break, and find something nutritious to eat?*

I notice I'm feeling sad and lonely—I acknowledge that I'd like some connection and support. *Would I be willing to go through my address book and place phone calls until I find someone to talk to? Would I be willing to go to a twelve-step meeting? Would I be willing to go for a hike?*

I notice I feel afraid and want more safety. *Would I be willing to walk away? Would I be willing to call for help? Would I be willing to express my honesty, my feelings, my needs, and a request?*

I notice I'm bored and wanting aliveness and adventure. *Would I be willing to go surfing? Would I be willing to play beach volleyball or go for a hike?*

I notice I'm feeling overwhelmed by the busyness of life, tired of doing the same thing over and over again. I want more aliveness, meaning, and clarity of direction. *Would I be willing to hop in the car and drive out of town? Would I be willing to head out to the mountains for some solitude with God?*

I notice my job is meeting my needs for support and flexibility, and I'm feeling grateful for that, but I'm also feeling uncomfortable and uneasy because I want to contribute to the well-being of others. *Would I be willing to go to an orphanage and play with the kids? Would I be willing to lead a small group or work on my book project?*

I feel joyful as my needs for connection are met. Would I be willing to express my honesty to this person? I ask myself if I could say something like *Susie, I'm so grateful for our time together. I'm feeling joyful in ways that I'm not used to expressing. I'm celebrating our connection this evening.*

I notice I'm feeling sad and lonely, and I acknowledge my needs for community and belonging. *Would I be willing to invite friends over for dinner to discuss forming a new small group? Would I be willing to search the Web for existing intentional communities and home-churches? Would I be willing to join an online dating site?*

Before moving on to the topic of empathy, I want to reemphasize that self-empathy is about listening to our heart so that we can be true to ourselves; listening and acknowledging what's really going on; and listening to our internal dialogue and making requests to meet our needs. We recognize that God, the source of all life, gave us our needs as a gift. By honoring this gift, we give honor to him and feel his love and caring, and we celebrate the spark of life and beauty within us.

As we go through the process of self-empathy, we begin to feel serenity and compassion. We are curious about the experience of others and we want to contribute to their well-being and share the bread of life that we are able to eat.[51] In the next chapter I discuss ways I can share the empathy I've received with other people as an act of love.

Being Empathetic with Someone Else

Earlier I listed a few qualities of children. They are open and vulnerable, and they freely express their needs. I now consider the qualities of being a parent, which parallels the role of the Compassionate Samaritan. A parent might have these thoughts about his child.

- I love hiom, and I want to meet his needs.
- I have an unexplainable desire to contribute to his well-being.
- I want to teach him the wisdom I've accumulated so far.

- I want to protect him and keep him safe.
- I am often tired; I need more rest. Parenting can be exhausting.
- I am sometimes overwhelmed by his incessant needs.
- I am sometimes embarrassed by his honesty, for I want to show respect to others.
- I sometimes tell myself that his needs are in conflict with my own.
- I wish the public education system were more in harmony with my values.
- I feel concern about my son's being heard and respected by other adults.
- I'm sometimes torn between different strategies in the heat of the moment.

As a parent, there is something inside me that makes me want to contribute to my son's well-being. Parents might differ on strategies, but at the level of needs we have a lot in common. Sometimes my own pain has interfered with parenting. After learning more about self-empathy, I find that I'm better able to meet my son's needs because I'm fully aware of my own. If I'm not, I might talk with friends, other parents, or a counselor to clarify what's going on.

Once I recognize my needs and connect with them, I can be with my son and help him clarify his needs. Being self-empathetic must come before offering empathy to someone else, otherwise we risk meeting neither our needs nor those of the other person.

When it comes to empathy, we can't give what we don't have. I find it helpful to think of empathy as a state one is in, not something that is done. At the same time, it's helpful to keep in mind that it's the needs of the other person that are being considered in the moment. Empathy is a gift offered to the person whose needs are on the table.

So in everything, do to others what you would have them do to you, for this sums up the Law and the Prophets. (Matthew 7:12, NIV)

These words of Jesus are often called the Golden Rule. I interpret it as meaning "consider each other's needs."[52] The following example demonstrates my point.

I am giving you a roasted pig because I'd like a roasted pig (even though you happen to be a vegetarian).

Of course, Jesus wasn't referring to strategies in the Golden Rule; he was referring to considering each other's needs and helping each other find ways to meet them. To follow the Golden Rule means empathizing with others. We all need to be heard, to be known, to be understood, to be treated with respect and consideration. We need to be valued as unique beings, created in the image and likeness of God.

When we offer empathy, we value the basic needs for respect and consideration at the same time we're present for another person and listening for their needs. Empathy is a gift that can be fully given after we've removed our plank. We can be aware and self-connected because our own need for empathy has been met. We become present enough to share our empathy with someone else.

As a result of self-empathy, we begin to feel a natural peace, curiosity, and compassion toward the person across from us. This curiosity can take any of several forms. We do know, however, what empathy is not. It isn't any of the following.[53]

- Giving advice: I think you should ...
- One-upping: That's nothing; wait till you hear my story.
- Educating: Okay, here's what you need to know.
- Consoling: It wasn't your fault; you did your best.
- Storytelling: That reminds me of the time when ...
- Shutting down: Cheer up! Don't feel so bad. Don't be sad.
- Interrogating: What happened? Then what did she say?

- Explaining: I would have called, but...
- Correcting: That's not how it happened.
- Sympathizing: Oh, you poor thing. I feel so _____ when you_____.

Sympathy is often confused with empathy. Sympathy means that the listener takes on the feelings of the other person, while empathy is about acknowledging the other person's experience.

The strategies listed above shift the focus from the other person back to us. I am not saying that these things are wrong or bad; they have their place in conversation. Sometimes it's important to ask questions to clarify what the other person is saying or to offer our honesty. These strategies are listed to show what empathy is and what it is not in NVC. Empathy is worth an extended discussion, because it's about exploring the heart of God within us and allowing ourselves to embrace it fully, finding the freedom we seek, and sharing our presence and grace with another person.

Marshall Rosenberg has said that empathy in NVC is a respectful presence with another person, which when verbalized invites the other person to connect with their own heart. Empathy is shared in a spirit of caring and curiosity for the experience of the other person. The intent of empathy is giving and connecting.

Although it can take on many forms in casual conversation, a classic empathetic statement sounds like *Are you feeling* _____ *because you need* _____? This empathetic question invites self-connection and addresses both feelings and needs. As the conversation flows back and forth, our needs for empathy and those of the other person are met. It is a form of grace, a gift that is freely given. In NVC, we acknowledge that often we give to others in order to meet our own need to contribute. This contribution comes directly from the heart of God, and we share it with all people. When giving empathy, we are aware of our own needs first, and then we try to guess at the needs of others. It's a guess, because we don't know for sure until we ask and they are willing to share.

The reason we guess at what the other person is feeling and needing is that if we were to assume we knew what they were experiencing, they would feel annoyed because their need for autonomy is not met. They would likely want the freedom to have their own experience and make their own choice to share their feelings or not. The motivation for giving empathy in NVC is to contribute to clarity, understanding, and connection, not to be right. For example, if I were to say *You're sad and you want respect!* – the other person might reply *Who made you God?* or *You don't know how I feel!*

Notice the use of the exclamation point in both the attempt at empathy and the response that shows how an aggressive posture usually elicits an aggressive posture in return. The connection is lost. The other person might be sad and want respect, just as I said, but the aggression interrupts the flow of connection. Thus it is important to remain open, present, and curious – like a child. If you want to establish empathy, guess at the other person's feelings and needs, and then check in to see if you're close.

The empathetic version of the conversation might be *Are you feeling sad because you need respect?* Here the feeling of sadness is tied to the need for respect when you talk about the other person's experience. You don't have to be right when you guess; your words are an invitation to the other person to look inside and see their own feelings and needs connected with their experience.

In NVC, empathy does not mean taking on the feelings of the other person, even though we might be moved by what we hear. Also, empathy doesn't require agreement. It's about acknowledging and witnessing the other person's life experience and providing support and caring so that they can see more clearly, connecting more deeply with the heart of God within. Empathy opens the door to a dialogue with our enemies.

Discussion

- From the list of actions that sound like empathy but are not, which do you find yourself doing most frequently? Do you agree that they have the potential to break the flow of conversation? Do you also see value in them, and if so, how?

- What is your understanding of Jesus's Golden Rule?

- How do you see the Golden Rule as important when giving empathy?

22.

Loving Our Enemies

Love your enemies. Pray for those who persecute you. (Matthew 5:44, NIV)

I'm curious—why would Jesus ask us to love our enemies and pray for them? What heart needs might be present in this request? It turns out there are a whole slew of them. In fact, without the ability to love our enemies, we'd have a hard time loving anyone, including ourselves, because when our needs are not met around someone in particular, it's likely we would label them and treat them as an enemy. Then we would blame them for our discomfort. When you do this, you make someone into an *enemy image.*

What comes up for me around enemy images? When I look inward, I quickly identify needs for safety, mutuality, peace, and harmony, and I want to contribute to meeting these needs. Also alive are the needs of the community, which are affected both directly and indirectly by violence. I begin to meet those needs by transforming myself and inviting others into a conversation that is life-giving and supported by the need for love; this transformation can also be a movement toward spiritual growth.

Having talked about the meaning of love and empathy as a form of grace, it seems appropriate to go back and consider our enemies. When Jesus said *love your enemies,* he wasn't asking us to have fuzzy, warm feelings toward them, nor did he ask us to agree with them. Empathy is a way to love my enemies by engaging them in dialogue about their experience, inviting them into their hearts, and opening the door for them to our own hearts through honest expression.

Giving honesty to people we label as our enemies is difficult and requires a great deal of discipline and practice. When working to drive out enemy images we've created, we must first come to terms with our own tendency to label someone as an enemy, or as evil, incompetent, or stupid. How do we do this? Through self-empathy. For example, every now and then as I'm driving on the freeway in Los Angeles, someone will cut me off. My thoughts might go something like this.

That idiot incompetent SOB, he can't drive worth a damn! Is that a woman or a man? That driver should be punished!

I realize that I'm stimulated by the person's driving and I hear what I'm telling myself about them. As I give myself empathy, I notice what's going on in my mind, and I might ask myself some questions.

Am I angry because I need more space, respect and consideration? Am I scared because I need safety? Am I concerned for my health and that of the people around me? Am I annoyed because I want justice?

I continue this process until I notice a mood change and begin feeling curious and compassionate about the other person. After some level of self-connection, it's helpful to guess at what's going on for them. After receiving enough self-empathy, my curiosity might sound something like this.

I wonder why they're in a hurry? Maybe they have a family emergency and want to help. Or maybe they're running late for work and concerned about their job and about supporting themselves. Maybe they're late for a party and are hungry for connection.

Driving on the highway, I can't know what's going on for the other person. The important thing is to deal with my own internal dialogue and to explore what's behind my labels and judgments. This points to the truth that we can't control others. Whether we like it or not, people have free will. We—and they—have the freedom and opportunity to behave according to our own needs and values.

Once we're clear about what's going on inside, we can formulate a strategy for moving forward. We might choose to write down the make of the car and the license plate number and report the incident to the police.

In other situations, when the other person is within talking distance—for example, when a person that just arrived skips to the front of a line—we could tell them what's going on to meet our needs for self-respect and honesty, provided we remain self-connected. It's important to be aware of our motivation and the need that is alive for us in our desire to tell the other person about our experience.

If I find I'm still angry and wanting to teach them a lesson, and I'm aware of it, I can tell I need more self-empathy. To talk with someone from this posture would likely lead to conflict. Marshall Rosenberg calls this *violent communication.* Given where I am in my journey, if I sensed that I was angry, I would find ways to deal with my emotions that are more likely to lead to everyone's needs being met without violence. Early on, when I was finding my voice and speaking my own truth, I did so in ways that met my need for expression, but usually at the expense of other people's needs for respect, consideration, and mutuality. This time in my life taught me many valuable lessons.

Loving our enemies begins with transforming our enemy images through self-empathy. We are now free and curious about the experience of the other human being. We are present for them so long as our needs for safety, consideration, and respect are being met. Sometimes God helps us meet those needs while in a difficult situation. It takes a lot of practice and discipline to stay in empathy around people we have labeled as enemies, but the payoffs are tremendous once we make this internal shift.

If we happen to make a judgment and hear ourselves doing it, we don't have to judge ourselves. We can choose to guess at the feelings and needs behind our judgment. We will know we have enough empathy when we feel curiosity and compassion toward ourselves and others. We can choose to guess at the other person's feelings and needs, knowing that they may not be used to looking inside themselves for the cause of their discomfort. It may be scary or painful for them to do so and they may choose not to do it.

If our attempts at empathy with others are effective, then connection is possible. It may also be that connection is not possible at this time with this person. We might not have been as self-connected as we would have liked, or we might have chosen words that stimulated the other person in undesirable ways. We might feel regret afterward, but this is part of the process of communication.

The important thing is to have an intention to connect and to let go of the outcome. If the other person is able to look inside, and you notice a shift in their mood, then it may be time to move into giving your honesty.

Discussion

- What is your understanding of loving your enemies?
- Who in your life do you label as an enemy?
- Do you have opportunities in your life to love your enemies?
- What makes loving your enemies difficult?

Protective Use of Force

There are times when our attempts at connection aren't working, or we are in imminent danger from the actions of another person. We have done what we can to take care of our plank, but there is still a danger that we or someone close to us will be harmed. This is the time for the protective use of force. We take immediate action, using only the amount of force needed to restore safety and to protect the threatened person from harm. Here are four examples.

- When Alex was a toddler, he loved life and explored freely. Once when we were at a park, about to leave, he ran out into the parking lot right in front of a car. In a split second, I jumped in front of the car and forcibly removed him from its path. I acted for his safety without consulting him, and I was willing to put my life on the line for his.

- My friends Brian and Julie have two daughters: Sierra, three, and Sage, six months. Sierra was pulling Sage's ear, and I pointed out the situation to Julie, who forcibly removed Sierra's hand.

- When I was in second grade in Puerto Rico, two boys approached me behind a local hangout. One of them, the smaller one, went behind me and grabbed me by the neck while the other approached me from the front. The kid behind me was saying something like, "Punch him in the stomach! Hurry up! That'll teach him!"

  I was startled and confused, not knowing who these kids were or why they were attacking me. At first I thought they were playing, so I decided to play their game. I reached behind my neck, grabbed the kid's hands, and shifted my weight to the left with my knees bent. When I pulled down hard over my right shoulder, he flipped over me onto his back. I was startled and so was he. I had never done such a thing before. The boy just lay there on his back with the wind knocked out of him. His friend stepped back and said nothing. I stood quietly, wondering what was next, still thinking it was part of a game. As the smaller boy got up, his friend said, "¡Vámonos! El sabe karate." ("Come on, let's go! He knows karate.")

As they turned the corner around the building, the younger one said, "¡Gringo, salte de mi país!" ("Gringo, get out of my country!")

It wasn't until then that I realized they intended to hurt me. I'm now guessing that they were expressing some pain they inherited from their parents—not genetically, but a story passed down through generations. I'm guessing their comments were expressing some pain around the results of the Spanish-American War, in which the United States took control of the island and their ancestors' needs for autonomy, freedom, safety, and mutual respect were not met. Or perhaps, it could be that their needs for financial support were not being met, and they blamed "gringos." I would love to someday find out.

- Also in Puerto Rico, my father formed a neighborhood watch group in response to some break-ins. My neighbors, my family, and I felt safe and comfortable in Dad's presence because he had police training in the Air Force and currently worked with a commission to reduce crime through community involvement programs. My father also owned a large revolver to help protect us. One morning our neighbors across the street called my dad at 2:00 AM, saying, "Some people broke into our shop—please help us!"

They were scared for their safety and wanted help to protect themselves and their means of support. My dad surprised the men and held them at gunpoint until the police arrived.

These and other events helped me feel safe because my needs for protection were met. Now that I have more awareness and compassion, I'm curious about those two men. Had they broken into our neighbors' house to feed their families, or had they done it to support a drug habit? Why did they want their needs met so badly that they risked violence and imprisonment?

NVC supports the use of force when all other means for a peaceful resolution have been exhausted and the life and safety of those close to us are at risk. This concept is extended to countries by applying *just war criteria*, which Walter Wink discusses at length in *The Powers That Be: Theology for a New Millennium.*

Now that we have discussed self-empathy for ourselves, empathy for people once viewed as enemies, and the protective use of force, we are ready to transition into honesty.

Discussion

- What is your reaction to this chapter? What feelings and needs are stimulated?
- How important is the protective use of force to you?
- Can you identify with the examples listed? If so, how?

23.

Honesty as Truth

If you follow my teachings, then you are really my disciples. Then you will know the truth and the truth will set you free. (John 8:31–32, NIV)

I have heard these verses used in many contexts, some of which were not in harmony with my values or my understanding of the intent of Jesus. The issue revolved around the interpretation of the word *truth*. I have heard the word used to judge and evaluate others with respect to the judger's point of view. A judger might call someone "bad" and accuse them of not following the rules as the judger understands them; they can decide to criticize for any reason, or no reason. Constant criticism doesn't change people's minds. It is crystal clear to me in these cases that the connection is broken and probably had never been there in the first place, for love is not present.

This chapter is about the counterpart to empathy, which is honesty. Focusing the search for truth by starting with ourselves is a way to discover a greater truth that is revealed by the Holy Spirit. We focus on the means, instead of the destination. Honesty follows self-empathy, where we become clear about the truth of our experience. In giving honesty, we describe our experience and our interpretation of life. We find that these steps are more effective in supporting the quality of connection that we desire in our hearts; metaphorically, we describe what the *plank* was hiding. If we can communicate this truth so that the other person can fully absorb and understand what we say, we will experience freedom as a result. In NVC, honesty is expressed by

Expressing an observation,
Naming the feelings that were stimulated,
Revealing the needs the feelings address, and
Making a request of the listener.

As noted earlier, observations, feelings, needs, and requests are called OFNR in NVC.

When we are ready to give honesty, we are fully aware of our own experience because we have received enough self-empathy to remove the obstacle that was blocking our self-awareness. We may have given the other person empathy and then noticed a shift in their attitude and body posture. Offering our honesty to the other person can keep the flow of conversation alive. We might say something like, "After listening to what you just told me, I have some things stirring inside me. Would you like to hear them?"

It's important to give the other person space to express their feelings fully before shifting to honesty.[54] They may have more to say, but if they don't, it might be a good time to continue with the request. I find that asking before giving one's honesty is important, especially when I don't know the other person well. If I do know them and we've been talking for a good while, I might choose to give my honesty without asking. It would sound something like "I'm really touched by what I just heard. I'm inspired by the meaning behind your story. How do you feel when you hear me say that?"

The feelings expressed were *touched* and *inspired,* and the need expressed was for *meaning.* Notice that a request immediately follows the feelings and needs and invites the other person to express how it was for them to receive our honesty. We will discuss the importance of requests later.

We may also want to express our not-so-pleasant feelings to the other person. When the other person has a propensity to hear honesty as a judgment, we might say something like, "I have some things going on inside. I'm worried that you'll hear them as criticism, but they're really about me. Would it be okay if I shared them with you?" We hope the other person says yes. If they say no, we could choose to give empathy, to leave, to call a friend, or to respond in some other way that meets needs for mutual respect.

A friend might have arrived later than our agreed upon time, and I'd say something like, "We had an agreement to meet for dinner at 7:00, and you arrived at 7:45. I'm feeling annoyed because I really value my time and would enjoy knowing that you do too. Would you be willing to tell me what you just heard me say?"

Sometimes the other person resists telling you what they heard, saying something like, "I heard you!" Then I might say, "I really value our relationship. I'm afraid you're hearing a judgment, and I want to know that I'm heard. Would you please tell me what you understood me to say?"

Sometimes the other person hears what we say, other times they don't. I'm surprised how often people say they heard me and yet reply with a judgment when we're listening for them to repeat the intent behind the need-words *consideration, respect,* or *value.*

After hearing the needs repeated, we might say, "Thanks for hearing me. I'm starting to relax a bit. I value our friendship enough to be honest with you. I'm wondering what's going on with you as you hear me say this?"

The last request is important, because it indicates how the conversation can flow. The other person might then give us their honesty as we switch roles again. It might sound something like this: "I'm feeling a little sad at hearing what you just said because I too value our friendship. I was talking to my mother, who's been ill, and I was so involved in the conversation that I lost track of time."

Now that they've given their honesty, we want to empathize with what we just heard: "I hear that you're sad and that you also value our friendship." Then they might say, "Yes, I was connecting with my mother in the hospital, and ..."

A conversation that flows back and forth between empathy and honesty can help meet both people's needs for connection, especially when the flow is well balanced. I find that deep mutual understanding between two people manifests itself into something more than just our words.

Discussion

- What is your interpretation of the word *truth* in the verse at the beginning of the chapter?

- How does one experience freedom when one knows the truth?

- Have you experienced honesty as a form of truth that can set you free? If so, how?

- Do you have any discomfort around being honest with other people? Explain.

24.

Money Is a Strategy, Not a Need

No one can serve two masters. Either he will hate the one and love the other, or he will be devoted to the one and despise the other. You cannot serve both God and Money. Therefore I tell you, do not worry about your life, what you will eat or drink; or about your body, what you will wear. Is not life more important than food, and the body more important than clothes? (Matthew 6:24–25, NIV)

Jesus reminds us that money cannot meet our deepest needs. Much about our lives revolves around money, but why? Jesus talked about it often, and repeated how important it is to remain free of it while still using it. He didn't tell us not to use money, but to see that we have a choice to serve God instead, for this path will bring us eternal life in the Kingdom. The way to God is through our hearts. Jesus pointed out to us that money is a means to an end in life, not life itself. A path in service of the heart of God brings fulfillment, but money is an empty vessel that can trap us in an illusion.

Money is a strategy to help us meet our needs, not a need in itself. Like any other overused strategy, if we treat money as a need, we may lose our connection to the people around us and lose our heart in the process. Money in itself isn't bad; in fact, it's very useful. It helps meet our needs, but it is not required for all things. Many of my friends exchange goods and services without money. Many NVC trainers accept payment based on what people are able to give with joy for their services.

My favorite story about money happened at a mediation workshop facilitated by Jim and Jori Manske. They invited me to attend for free to support the local NVC community. I'm also guessing they enjoyed connecting with me, as we had met before at an international intensive training. I showed up and participated fully. At the end of the workshop, I wanted to contribute to them. I remembered a set of wind chimes of theirs that had deteriorated and broken due to weathering and age. After the workshop, I asked if they would like a new set of wind chimes, and they agreed. I went online and found a shop that made chimes tuned to various harmonies, asked Jim to select one, and then I had his choice shipped to his home in Albuquerque. Later I received this note from Jim.

> *Although the wind is calm here today, and thus our new chimes are resting in silence, I love knowing they're standing by outside my bedroom porch, ready to sing to me with the breeze. The sound is lovely and nourishing to my soul, and it's fun that their ring reminds me of you and the SoCal NVC community, ringing the bells of freedom through NVC.*

Several years later, at the end of a five-day retreat, Jim came up to me, gave me a good-bye hug, and said, "We've been away in Hawaii for several months. I've been longing for home and looking forward to the sound of the wind chimes you gave us."

I was moved by his words. I could tell he enjoyed my gift, and I had forgotten all about it. I said, "I'm really touched and grateful to hear that. Thanks for giving them back to me." He didn't physically give them back; we shared in the spirit of giving and receiving with our words and presence. We exchanged glances. My eyes got misty with celebration, and we went about our business. No money was exchanged, but something else was exchanged in its place. The transaction took place freely on both sides, meeting both our needs. Something about the gift seemed to have a life of its own, offering joy to both the giver and receiver — it went beyond the wind chimes.

That same spirit of giving and receiving can apply when money is exchanged. April in the United States is the time to account for income received in the previous year and pay income taxes. A part of me that wants autonomy and freedom to spend the money I earned in ways that directly meet my needs, but I also acknowledge the needs met by our collective agreements, which I sometimes take for granted.

- Clean water flowing from the faucet
- A sanitation system to take care of waste
- State and national park systems that protect natural resources and are affordable and available to everyone
- Freedom to speak, to express myself, and to write this book
- Freedom to vote for the selection of government officials
- Needs for safety, security, and order are met
- A system of government that is able to adapt to change while preserving the core values of a democratic system—including a balance of the powers of the executive, legislative, and judicial branches.

Of course, government does things I don't agree with, and I mourn the needs that are not met. But while I prepare, print, and mail my taxes, I celebrate the needs that are met as I pray for our government. It too needs the redemption of Christ.[55]

Discussion

- What is the meaning of money as you see it?
- Why do you think so much of our lives revolves around money?
- What is your understanding of the verses at the beginning of this chapter in Matthew 6:24–25?
- How do you treat money? What role does it play in your life?
- Do you see money as good, bad, or neutral? Discuss and support your point.

- Where is your wealth invested or geared toward serving? Where is your focus and emphasis placed most of the time?

- What is your interpretation of the following verses attributed to Jesus?

Do not store up for yourselves treasures on earth, where moth and rust destroy, and where thieves break in and steal. But store up for yourselves treasures in heaven, where moth and rust do not destroy, and where thieves do not break in and steal. For where your treasure is, there your heart will be also. (Matthew 6:19–21, NIV)

25.

Serving Others: Duty vs. Desire

Contributing to others is a beautiful heart need that we have often. It's important to be aware not only of our need for contribution, but of the needs of the other person as well. The other person may not be in a place to receive what we have to offer. To give something to someone that they may not want is not necessarily a gift; we are missing the mark if they don't receive our gift gratefully.

If they are unable or unwilling to receive what we have to offer, we can give ourselves empathy for not being able to contribute to our friend. Then we might step back and consider other needs that are alive for both of us. Seeking strategies that meet the needs of people on both sides of a relationship is something to be celebrated. There is nothing like the joy I feel when what I do meets my needs and those of the other person.

Then the King will say to those on his right, "Come, you who are blessed by my Father; take your inheritance, the kingdom prepared for you since the creation of the world. For I was hungry and you gave me something to eat, I was thirsty and you gave me something to drink, I was a stranger and you invited me in, I needed clothes and you clothed me, I was sick and you looked after me, I was in prison and you came to visit me."

Then the righteous will answer him, "Lord, when did we see you hungry and feed you, or thirsty and give you something to drink? When did we see you a stranger and invite you in, or needing clothes and clothe you? When did we see you sick or in prison and go to visit you?"

The King will reply, "I tell you the truth, whatever you did for one of the least of these brothers of mine, you did for me." (Matthew 25:34–40, NIV)

Early on in my spiritual walk, I was encouraged to serve others. Initially it felt like a drag, because I hadn't taken care of myself yet. I realized that I was thinking that I had to do this in order to be a good Catholic or a good Christian. This was the same dynamic I experienced in my intimate relationship, where I tried to buy a woman's love—by being *nice* all the time. Was I trying to buy my way into heaven? After a great deal of personal inventory work, I realized I was feeling discomfort around my motivation to serve. Was I doing service in order to buy God's love? I realized my actions were not in harmony with my heart, but I wasn't sure why or how.

As I got more involved in NVC, I heard Marshall Rosenberg mention that someone always pays a price when things are done out of duty or obligation, or to buy love. He gave the following example, which I have adapted to my own experience to make the point.

It's 2:00 AM and I'm fast asleep. Alex is crying in the crib next to our bed. It's my turn to feed him, but I'm tired. There are two ways to approach this situation.

I might pull myself up by my bootstraps, deny being tired, and get out of bed. I tell myself, *I'm not tired. I'll do anything for my son.* So I get up and feed him.

The second possibility is to acknowledge the truth of my experience. *I'm so tired I could sleep for a week. I haven't slept well in days; I need more rest.* As I honor my feelings, I begin to feel compassion for Alex. *I'm sure he's feeling scared and hungry. Am I able to get up and see how he's doing? I think so.* "Hey, buddy, are you hungry?" I pick him up. "Let me get you a bottle, okay?" I carry him to the kitchen for his feeding.

Notice the length of the two paragraphs. The first one is brief and effective. The second is longer and takes more effort and awareness, since I'm acknowledging the experience of two or three people (me, my wife, and my son). The second takes discipline; the first is a reaction. I notice that I'm less able to be compassionate when I am tired, hungry, or lonely. I'm less able to connect with others and behave in loving ways if my own needs aren't being met. But I acted even though I needed rest, and I only acknowledged my need for rest when I gave myself empathy.

I have noticed that empathy, toward both myself and others, gives me power. The Holy Spirit provides something that wasn't there before. Empathy opens the door for God to provide spiritual food almost instantaneously. In recovery circles, these mantras are repeated over and over again:

Be True to Yourself.
Take Care of Yourself.

It is by honoring the truth of our experiences that we are able to love and connect with others. We must take care of our own plank before contributing to the needs of others, before clearing the speck from someone else's eye. When we take care of ourselves, we are in a better position to serve others, and act with integrity — I contribute when it's alive for me; otherwise I don't. I have noticed that after self-empathy, I am more likely to contribute to others while being in integrity — I feel joy as a result of giving while being true to myself.

Once I've given myself enough self-empathy and understanding, how do I know if I'm actually contributing? Ask first and check in afterward. I know that I frequently feel annoyed when someone tries to contribute something to me and I don't want it. I interpret their actions as preaching or fixing. I feel annoyed because I want consideration for my own experience and for my own needs. I want my need for autonomy to be respected. I'd like to be asked before someone does something for me, in case I don't want it.

This is more of a suggestion than a rule. My experience is different when I know the other person well. Sometimes the check-in isn't necessary. Either way, if someone tries to give me something I don't want, I can give them empathy and honesty, which may sound something like, "You seem excited to contribute something to me, but right now I'm not up to receiving solutions. I just want to be heard. Would you be willing to listen to me for the time being?" Ideally, they reply with something like, "So you just want to be heard?"

In this case I might say something like, "Yes, I hear that you'd like to help me out. But right now, I'd like for you to hear me. Your listening will help me get clear with my own stuff. Are you willing to listen for ten more minutes?"

Sometimes a friend will have a difficult time hearing honesty; they might interpret it as criticism or judgment, and responses to perceived criticism and judgment can be as diverse as the grains of sand on a beach. As an example, they might say something like, "You don't want my help? Fine, forget you!" or "I'm just trying to help! What's wrong with you?" or "You're just complaining about your problem. Why don't you just fix it?"

If our friend's response is something like these, we could give them emergency empathy—brief acknowledgments of their experience—followed by a restatement of our honesty. Here's what emergency empathy might sound like: "Are you hurt because you'd really like to help? As you listen to me tell my story, are you frustrated because you want peace and harmony?"

When giving empathy, it's not important to be right. It's best to express it as a question. Having an intention of love and understanding is important. If your empathy is a little off, your friend will give you more information, or you might have to do more guessing. Sometimes your friend might be so disconnected from their own heart that they are unable to engage in this kind of conversation. The reality is that connecting with people can be difficult and is not always possible. Not everyone chooses to connect to their hearts or to connect with others.

My current growth challenge is to remain self-connected in the midst of judgment and disconnection, and to extend compassion and understanding even in the midst of heated rhetoric and confrontation. I believe that that by staying connected to my heart, I stay connected to God, allowing the Holy Spirit to work.

Discussion

- What is your understanding of service? Do you give service to others? Why or why not?

- Have you been involved in service projects? What are they?

- In the story of the baby crying at 2:00 AM, what is the difference between the two approaches? Which option is more comfortable for you and why?

- What do you think is God's message for you regarding service?

- Was there a time when you tried to contribute to someone else, but your attempt wasn't well received? What was it like for you?

26.

Expressing Gratitude as a Celebration

The Kingdom of Heaven can be illustrated by the story of a king who prepared a great wedding feast for his son. When the banquet was ready, he sent his servants to notify those who were invited. But they all refused to come, and he said to his servants, "The wedding feast is ready, and the guests I invited aren't worthy of the honor. Now go out to the street corners and invite everyone you see." (Matthew 22:2–3, 8–9, NLT)

Gratitude is like a feast, we are all invited to attend. There is an abundance of food and drink, and yet we often find reasons not to go. The world gets in the way and so does the fruit of the Tree of Judgment. Evaluations and criticism keep us from the banquet of gratitude.

Gratitude is a feeling that naturally arises after needs are met, and because it feels so good, we want the other person to know it. The motivation for showing gratitude could be celebration. Traditionally, people just say thank you and are done with it. Other times, people choose to give their evaluations, which might sound something like this.

That was good! You did a good job.
You are awesome!
This is better than _____.
You are the best _____ I know.

NVC invites us to consider an alternative to giving evaluations or just saying thanks. Gratitude may be expressed richly by saying specifically what the other person did that we liked so much and then telling them what we feel and what needs are being met. I've noticed that hearing gratitude triggers self-critical thinking for many people, and it can get in the way of receiving the gift being offered. Self-critical thinking may be spoken aloud or silently in words such as these.

It was nothing.
No problem.
It really wasn't that good.
You don't have to thank me; I would have done it anyway.
It's not as good as Joe's invention.
It was my duty.

Notice how easily the inner critic can steal the joy from gratitude. Because I want to contribute to their celebration with my gratitude and get past their self-critical thinking, I make a point of asking them to tell me what they heard me say — I make a request. Such gratitude could sound something like this.

Ever since you painted my room, I've felt inspired because I love the cleanliness and beauty of my surroundings. Just to make sure you hear how happy I am, would you be willing to tell me what you just heard me say? Or

I'm curious — what is your experience at hearing this?

That massage you gave me was fabulous! I feel relaxed, open, cared for, and connected to you. I really like how you touch me. Would you tell me what I just said? Or

How are you feeling after hearing this?

I'm really appreciating the color and aroma of this meal. The red of the peppers contrasted with the salad greens, and the basic brown rice and black beans, form a cauldron of delight! The aroma rises up with the steam and fills me with anticipation. Not only is it beautiful and fragrant, but I know your natural ingredients and the love you put into it nourish my body and my soul. Thank you. Just to make sure you heard me, would you tell me what you heard? Or

How was it for you to hear what I just said?

Having the heart and intention of gratitude is most important. Following the OFNR formula is not always necessary, but it is helpful in identifying the elements that facilitate a deeper connection. When I describe to the other person the specifics of what they did that I liked so much, they're better able to relate to what I'm saying. By naming the feelings that are stimulated and the needs that are met, they can more fully celebrate their contribution to me. The request can be used to reinforce the celebration within the person receiving the gratitude.

Discussion

- Do you experience gratitude as evaluation in your life— do people say *Good job!* to you? How do you feel when that happens?
- How do you express gratitude? How does it feel?
- What forms of gratitude do you find most fulfilling?
- Why do you think people express gratitude in words of evaluation?

27.

Conversation of Forgiveness

For if you forgive men when they sin against you, your heavenly Father will also forgive you. (Matthew 6:14, NIV)

In this chapter we explore the elements of forgiveness, showing that it starts with self-empathy. After we've taken the time to work on ourselves, we can approach others and extend the spirit of forgiveness to them. The Parable of the Unforgiving Debtor shows that giving forgiveness doesn't necessarily teach the receiver to forgive others but that self-empathy can free the heart and make it possible to forgive. Jesus said that you must "forgive your brother from your heart" (Matthew 18:21–35, NIV).

The most poignant example of forgiveness in my life relates to my relationship with my dad. In this chapter I tell how NVC helped me to forgive him and connect with him before he passed away. The conversation of forgiveness lasted several years, and I spent most of the time working on it within myself before I started talking to Dad about it.

I experienced a lot of violence when I was a kid, with much physical violence from my father. I have painful memories from my childhood, and I know my parents had painful memories from their childhoods. Their pain affected the way they parented me and my sister and how they treated each other. I mention this not to judge them or to play a victim of circumstance, but because it influenced my life, my first and only marriage, and my personal growth that took place later on.

My father used to hit me with his belt or his fraternity paddle. He would chase me around the house and hit me when he caught me. One day I was playing with my friends in the front yard and suddenly I felt someone grab me by the hair and pull me toward the house. It took me a few moments to realize that it was my dad dragging me home for dinner.

I witnessed my parents yelling at each other in anger and slapping each other in the face. I remember sitting at the kitchen counter and soaking it all in, feeling scared and confused. For the longest time, I couldn't understand or put into words my feelings toward my dad. I was angry and hurt, and I dealt with it by journaling, counseling, going to twelve-step meetings, and avoiding my father.

Today I can identify the feelings and needs that were not met when my father treated me the way he did. After a long process of self-empathy, I found these, among others.

I felt hurt because I wanted more support and caring.
I was angry because my needs for safety and protection were not met.
I felt disappointed because I wanted respect and consideration.
I was frustrated and wanted to be heard and understood.
I felt sadness because I needed to be valued, celebrated, and loved.

To forgive, one must have this kind of internal dialogue and let it soak in. Self-empathy is the path to forgiveness. I spent time journaling and meditating around my needs and how they weren't met during my childhood. I don't say that I was abused, neglected, or misunderstood; those evaluative words would have kept me stuck in judgment, blame, and victimhood. Now I just observe my feelings and guess at my needs.

Through reflection and prayer, I saw that my needs had an inherent beauty to them. They pointed to something I had in my heart, even in the midst of the violence, that spoke of God's love for me in my needs for freedom, play, support, caring, safety, protection, mutuality, respect, consideration, to be heard and understood, and to be valued, celebrated, and loved.

My path to healing and recovery comes from acknowledging the truth of my experience and connecting to the love of God in my heart. This process of healing took time and a lot of work. The good news is that I got to a place of forgiveness while Dad was still alive. I had the opportunity to talk to him about my experiences and about my needs that were met and not met. I was able to have this conversation with him from a place of love and compassion because I had already forgiven him in my heart.

Dad had pulmonary fibrosis, a fatal lung disease, and was hospitalized at the University of Washington Medical Center in Seattle. When I first arrived at the hospital, I tried to hide my feelings and act *strong, like a man*. I soon realized it was taking too much energy to fake strength, so I decided to be fully present instead. I cried, letting my tears flow when they came up. I was guessing that this kind of emotional honesty was new for him, especially coming from a man. I was relieved to be able to be myself, though, and my father seemed to accept me – and my honesty – when I came to visit him.

Some time during that week, I asked Dad for his words of wisdom, for the most important concept that he had learned and that he wanted to pass on to me. He simply said, "Respect." I had heard this message many times throughout my life, in various contexts – his one word sentence was just a reminder.

I had the opportunity to reminisce with him about good times we had together and to share my gratitude with him. Here are some of the things we celebrated in his hospital room.

- One of my earliest memories of Dad was a time when he came home from work and lifted me up on his lap.

I remember the warmth and caring I felt as we napped together on his recliner.

- My dad taught me how to hit a golf ball; he even made me custom clubs. He spent a lot of time teaching me how to do it right. I remember the encouragement I felt, hearing him acknowledge my skill as we hit balls in our backyard over the fence and into the woods.

- One of my favorite childhood adventures was when Dad and I climbed the backyard fence into the woods with our BB rifle and went exploring for several hours. I remember walking between the trees, asking if we could shoot the rifle, and taking a few shots at old tree stumps. I still have dreams of that adventure, and how excited and nervous I was, but I felt safe because my dad was with me.

- The two of us went to Puerto Rico ahead of my mom and sister to open up our new house in Bayamón. We slept on the floor, and the next day we went around the neighborhood exploring the half-built houses. I remember feeling respected, important enough to accompany him to Puerto Rico. This was my first extended trip alone with Dad, and it will always be with me.

- One of my fondest memories of exploring with Dad took place on the *finca*, our family's plot of land in Puerto Hermina, in his hometown of Quebradillas, Puerto Rico. We went hiking and soon found an ancient artifact that looked like a stone weapon. We explored caves that led to an opening in a cliff wall overlooking a canyon, about sixty feet off the ground. There were giant tree vines extending out of the cave and working their way down to the canyon floor. After climbing about ten feet down, we came upon a large bees' nest and honeycomb. The bees were swirling all around the nest but seemed not to notice us. We continued climbing down and eventually walked all the way to the ocean.

- My dad often encouraged me to do well in school and to get involved in sports. He and Mom worked hard to pay for my private education in Catholic schools.

- I am grateful that Dad and I played basketball every day for our last four years in Puerto Rico. He taught me how to pass, how to dribble the ball, and his trademark hook shot—which I learned and used successfully against kids that were taller than me. We usually played on the same team against other kids from our neighborhood; we had special plays where we'd pass each other the ball and score. We won a lot of games together. Recently I celebrated his gift to me by beating my uncle Mike at one-on-one.

- When I was in high school, my dad, encouraged by my uncle Ruben, got me a five-piece drum set so that I could be in a rock and roll band.

In his hospital room, Dad asked for more oxygen. I paused for a moment and then found the courage to say, "Dad, we're giving you all we've got. We can't turn it up any more." He didn't say anything; neither did I. There was nothing to say. Later on, the doctor examined him, she said, "If you were meaning to have any conversations, now is the time for them." I was the only visitor that afternoon, and I settled in to talk with Dad, just the two of us. I took his hand and said something like this.

"Dad, I have some regret around my distance from you after your divorce from Mom. I'm sad that we lost so much time. I was confused and needed space to figure things out."

"I'm sad about that too," he said. "That was a really difficult time." He shared some of his regrets with me. "When you were younger, I wish I had been more loving."

I said, "Dad, I forgive you for all that, I really do."

We sat together quietly. His face was pained behind his oxygen mask. I cried.

I am grateful to have spent the last two weeks of Dad's life with him. A part of me healed as we talked. I'm torn between the joy of connecting with him and sadness that I waited so long, and I mourn that he is no longer here to talk with me, hang out, and hug. My experience of forgiving him has given me a sense of peace and calm around our relationship, as if the healing extended into the past, bringing restoration to my heart. I hope he's hearing my words so that he can celebrate how far we came together in our lives. Thanks, Dad!

Special Acknowledgment

I want to take this opportunity to express my deep gratitude to the doctors, staff, and volunteers at the University of Washington Medical Center. The volunteers in the ICU greeted me and gave me useful information, and they were usually around to help us out. The nurses were skilled, professional, caring, and concerned. Dr. Ragu and Dr. Shai, researchers in pulmonary fibrosis, went out of their way to talk with us about Dad's condition, taking hours of time to explain how quickly he was deteriorating in language we could understand. Dr. Shai even took us into the research lab to show us a comparison of his MRI results with those from two years before, which helped us to see into Dad's condition and appreciate his challenges.

I especially want to acknowledge Dr. Anne Loge for her empathy and honesty in a difficult situation. The clear information she gave me helped me to be present with my father when it counted the most. She and her staff met my needs for support in a way that gave me hope, not for curing Dad, but hope for humanity. They demonstrated the power of empathy by their presence, their words, their focus on the needs of patients and family members—all powerful and life-giving.

I celebrate their contributions to me, to my family, and to the greater family of humanity in everything they do. Thank you for all your efforts, seen and unseen.

The next chapter focuses on the process of forgiveness as set forth in Marshall Rosenberg's restorative justice programs.

Discussion

- What comes up for you after reading this story? What feelings and needs were stimulated?
- Does this chapter add to your understanding of forgiveness? How did the story help?
- What about the story captured your attention the most? Why?
- Did anything in the story make you uncomfortable? Why?

28.

Restorative Justice

"Teacher, this woman was caught in the act of adultery. In the Law, Moses commanded us to stone such women. Now what do you say?" They were using this question as a trap, in order to have a basis for accusing him.

But Jesus bent down and started to write on the ground with his finger. When they kept on questioning him, he straightened up and said to them, "If any one of you is without sin, let him be the first to throw a stone at her." Again he stooped down and wrote on the ground.

At this, those who heard began to go away one at a time, the older ones first, until only Jesus was left, with the woman still standing there. Jesus straightened up and asked her, "Woman, where are they? Has no one condemned you?"

"No one, sir," she said. "Then neither do I condemn you," Jesus declared. "Go now and leave your life of sin." (John 8:4-11, NIV)

Here Jesus reminds us to let go of the role of judge and our desire to punish those who fall short of our standards. He reminds us that everyone has sinned, missed the heart of God. Our job is to try to make the mark, perhaps by having conversations about the mark, and for those who are open to receiving it, to encourage others to do the same through love. Jesus invites us to help those in need in order to restore our connection with God and each other.

Marshall Rosenberg, the originator of Nonviolent Communication, speaks often about his Restorative Justice programs, which offer a model for how forgiveness and redemption can occur between people who are at odds. He works with victims and perpetrators of crimes in a correctional facility, helping them to hear each other. The perpetrators are there because they broke the law, violating the common agreements of our society.

There are two sides to the perpetrator; recognizing both and reconciling them is important to helping them connect to their hearts.

- The *Educator*, their inner critic, wants to teach them something about their actions—it wants to contribute to their learning. They judge themselves for what they have done.

- The *Chooser* opted to do something to meet their immediate needs, which broke the law, perhaps causing harm to other people.

Restorative justice is used to reconnect people to their hearts and to other people in order to find the mutual understanding that is needed for forgiveness and peace. Here we discuss how Restorative Justice works with perpetrators and victims, but the process can be applied to any situation in which someone's needs were met at the expense of the needs of another.

As you may recall, my roommate Mark was the victim of violence by someone he knew. The blows to his head were sudden and unexpected, occurring after he spoke candidly to an old acquaintance. In an imaginary conversation, I use this story as an example to demonstrate the process.

Dr. Rosenberg's Restorative Justice process,[56] greatly simplified, follows these steps.

Empathy for the Victim

- The victim speaks freely to the perpetrator, relating how his or her life was affected by the actions of the perpetrator.
- The facilitator gives empathy to the victim by listening and, in our example, helping the victim identify feelings and needs that were not met. Mark, as the victim, might experience feelings such as these—with the help of an NVC facilitator:

  I have scars that make me look unattractive, and I feel hurt.

  I'm concerned about my medical bills—I feel financially vulnerable.

  I feel sad because my needs for respect, safety, and mutuality were not met.

- The facilitator asks the perpetrator to tell what they heard the victim say. The facilitator quite often must guide the perpetrator toward hearing the victim's needs. In this case, Mark's needs are respect, safety, and mutuality.

Mourning the Needs of the Educator

- After the victim feels sufficiently heard, the facilitator shifts to the perpetrator and asks, "How do you feel when you hear [the victim] say that?"

  The perpetrator usually replies with self-judgment, saying things like "I did something really stupid" or "I'll never amount to anything." The facilitator then helps the perpetrator become aware of the feelings and needs that are alive for them. This step might sound like this:

  > Facilitator: "When you tell yourself that you 'did something really stupid,' are you feeling some regret and wishing you would have had more clarity in the moment?"
  >
  > Perpetrator: "Yeah. And I wish I would have been able to communicate better."
  >
  > Facilitator: "So, you're feeling regret around how you expressed yourself?"
  >
  > Perpetrator: "Yeah. I'm so used to yelling and screaming when people don't agree with me that hitting someone seems natural."
  >
  > Facilitator: "Are you disappointed because you'd like to be able to show respect while expressing yourself?"
  >
  > Perpetrator: "Yeah, I wish I could talk like you do; it seems so easy when you do it."
  >
  > Facilitator: "So, you'd like more ease in communicating—you wish you were more skilled at it?" ...

  Marshall calls this *giving empathy to the educator*—acknowledging the voice within the perpetrator that presses them to learn from their actions.

- After helping the perpetrator get sufficiently clear with the needs of the Educator that were not met, the facilitator acknowledges and summarizes the needs identified. The victim is invited to acknowledge the needs of the perpetrator. With a little help from the facilitator, Mark, the victim, might say "I hear that he's feeling regret that his needs for showing respect were not met; he's wishing he was more skilled at communicating."

  The victim may have a hard time shifting gears as he listens to the perpetrator talk about his unmet needs. The facilitator might have to offer empathy to the victim to keep the dialogue moving.

- After the victim has heard the perpetrator's feelings and needs and the perpetrator feels heard, the facilitator might ask the victim how he feels after hearing what was said. Mark might say, "I'm feeling some relief now that my need for understanding is met."

Empathy with the Chooser

- After the perpetrator has received enough empathy for his Educator, it's time to give empathy to their Chooser. This helps the perpetrator identify the needs they were trying to meet when they committed the crime. There was a reason for what they did.

  It is a key step in the process of forgiveness to be able to identify the needs of the Chooser *without judgment*. Note that connecting to the needs does not imply approval of choices and strategies. With a little help, and several rounds of empathy, we might identify Mark's assailant's feelings and needs as *I was angry because I wanted some respect and to be valued, and now I feel sad because I miss your friendship and companionship.*

- The facilitator asks the victim to tell the perpetrator the needs that were alive for them at the time of the crime. In our example, Mark might say, "I hear that he needed respect and to be valued and that he was missing our friendship."

  This process can be a catharsis for the perpetrator when the victim acknowledges the truth of their experience at the time of the crime. This is also the time when forgiveness might take root in the heart of the victim and when healing begins to take place in the heart of the perpetrator.

Searching for Strategies

- After the victim and perpetrator have clarified the needs of the perpetrator at the time of the crime, the facilitator invites them to brainstorm together on alternative strategies to meet both their needs more effectively. The goal is to find ways to get their needs met while also meeting the needs of those around them and living consistently with the needs in their hearts.

- These are some strategies we might come up with to help Mark's assailant deal with his feelings and get his needs met more effectively.

  Breathe
  Take a timeout
  Go for a walk
  Find new friends
  Develop a hobby that encourages self-respect
  Enroll in an NVC workshop

The dialogue above is a synopsis of a process that might take hours, days, or years. It is offered as an example of how the process might work. The facilitator, who is trained in NVC, guides the conversation to make the connections easier by translating any judgments and thinking into the language of the heart—using feelings and needs as a means to clarity, understanding, and connection.

This type of restorative justice stands in stark contrast with the prevailing system of punitive justice. A conversation about the truth enables the love of Christ to redeem the conflicts between people and bring the peace of forgiveness. The punitive system of justice is based on the myth of redemptive violence, which says that redemption is achieved by punishing others.[57] Those who believe this myth think that making the perpetrator suffer will bring comfort to the victims and meet our societal need for justice. Locking people up in a cell may help meet the community's need for safety (or the illusion of safety), but by itself it offers the perpetrator no redemption with little chance for growth and for reentering society with tools that enable them to contribute their unique, God-given gifts and talents.

The process of Restorative Justice focuses on the needs of the heart that were missed, which we discussed earlier as sin—the needs that were met at the expense of another person's needs. By avoiding moral judgment of right or wrong and focusing instead on present and past needs, the dialogue enables both parties to find ways of living that are in harmony with each other through healing and learning. This harmony is of the heart and mind may continue even if the victim and perpetrator never see each other again. The healing and forgiveness that Restorative Justice provides them are timeless because an enduring kind of learning takes place for both sides.

Rather than condemning the perpetrator through moral judgment, if the two are able to engage in this kind of conversation, it gives the Holy Spirit a chance to help them discover the mutual understanding, love, and creativity needed to live in harmony with the gospel message of Jesus.

Discussion

- What comes up for you after reading this section?
- What is your understanding of the perpetrator's Chooser versus their Educator?
- In your opinion, how effective is the punitive system of justice? What needs are met and what needs are not met?
- Do you see a place for restorative justice in your city and state?

29.

Empathetic Role-Play

Restorative justice is a model for finding forgiveness. But what if the perpetrator or victim cannot take part in the conversation, perhaps due to geographic distance, mental or physical illness, or death?

The heart of the conversation can still take place through an empathetic role-play facilitated by someone trained in NVC such as a close friend, pastor, priest, therapist or some other counselor. Here the facilitator takes on the role of the missing person. They are assumed to be connected to their own heart (they are *resourced* through self-empathy) and able to offer empathy to the other person, acknowledging their feelings and needs.

A facilitator who knows something about the missing person's motivation, feelings, and needs might use that to complement the empathy with honesty so that the person present can better understand the other side. The source of the information might be letters, emails, reports, or interviews. If the information is not available, the facilitator might interview people involved to get a sense of the missing person's heart. It isn't crucial to get the facts exactly right. What is important is to facilitate a conversation of the heart with the person present, in order to bring their feelings and needs into their awareness so that the Holy Spirit can heal, redeem the brokenness, and make room for forgiveness.

I have personally experienced the power of this process, both as a participant and as a facilitator. I had the privilege of working with Marshall Rosenberg at an intensive training workshop, where I processed pain related to my separation, divorce, and distance from my son. I experienced four cathartic emotional releases, resulting in feelings of compassion and peace. I have also facilitated this process with family members estranged from their relatives. After completing the process, I celebrated hearing gratitude from the participants as my needs for contribution were met.

The process of empathetic role-play can be helpful to victims, perpetrators, members of the community, and friends and relatives on both sides. It can restore our hearts to a state of peace, harmony, and communion with God through the healing spirit of Christ.

Discussion

- What comes up for you as you read about empathetic role-play?

- Is it scary to consider a stranger role-playing someone who has harmed you? What feelings and needs are stimulated for you?

30.

Prayer as Conversation

And when you pray, do not be like the hypocrites, for they love to pray standing in the synagogues and on the street corners to be seen by men. I tell you the truth, they have received their reward in full. But when you pray, go into your room, close the door and pray to your Father, who is unseen. Then your Father, who sees what is done in secret, will reward you. (Matthew 6:5–6, NIV)

In this verse, Jesus points to the need for integrity through the metaphor of the hypocrites. The word *hypocrite,*[58] while not part of the Hebrew language, is part of the Greek language, meaning to feign or pretend. My interpretation is that Jesus meant it as a reference to actors in a play wearing masks—pretending to be something they are not. The implication is that something underneath is covered up; the face showing is different from the real one inside the mask. We can only guess at the motivation for those standing in the synagogue and on street corners to pray. Was it to be seen and heard? They were looking outside themselves for their reward in life, not for a true connection with God in their hearts. Jesus invites us to connect closely with God by opening our hearts with honesty, alone in our rooms.

Through prayer, God helps me get clear with the experience of my heart as I tell him what's going on as honestly as I know how. Afterward, I listen for his empathy. Jesus tells us, "your Father knows what you need before you ask him" (Matthew 6:8).

If God knows my needs already, then why pray at all? Because I may not know what I really need. I may be focused on worldly strategies to get what I *want* instead of what I *need*. Prayer is a way to clarify my needs and to find the truth in my experience. When Jesus said, "Give us today our daily bread" (Matthew 6:11) as part of the Lord's Prayer, he invited us to acknowledge our need to be fed and to express our gratitude as we eat both literal food and metaphorical food of the spirit: "Man does not live on bread alone, but on every word that comes from the mouth of God" (Matthew 4:4).

Prayer is nothing more than having a conversation with God. I experience prayers that involve "I" statements as authentically expressing my own words and intentions. I admit that sometimes I enjoy using "we" statements in prayer, but I oftentimes feel annoyed when I hear other people use them, as though they knew others' hearts. I prefer "I" statements because I value expressing myself rather than letting others speak for me.

At the same time, I have experienced the joy of having someone pray for me after hearing what is going on; their prayer puts my requests and intentions in their own words, letting me know that they heard and understood what I had said earlier—this is a form of empathy. This kind of prayer helps me to more clearly identify what is stirring in my heart and to visualize possibilities—I get to feel the comfort of the support and caring in their words.

We can talk with God in the same way we talk with one another. Perhaps God's feedback isn't the same as theirs, but the Holy Spirit can make itself known through other people. The intimate conversations we have with others can be viewed as a form of prayer.

Religious language, rituals, and structures are not required for prayer. Of course, there are times when we want to pray by writing poetry, singing, or even dancing, but we don't have to do any of these things. In the best case, we don't pray out of duty or obligation, and we don't want to buy a special favor from God. We do it because something in us wants to express itself. If we want to celebrate something, we can express our honesty in observations, feelings, needs, and even requests. We have absolute freedom in speaking to God. If we want to ask for something, we can make a request, or even make a demand; sometimes the answer that comes as a result of our prayer disallows our wants so that we can let go and connect more deeply to our heart and to the Holy Spirit within us.

There are times for mourning with God and others, expressing the grief and sadness of losing someone. After someone close to us transitions from this life, we might feel sad because we miss them. Our needs for connection and support from this person are no longer met. We miss talking to them and sharing our life experience with them. When losing a marriage partner of many years, our sadness can feel like despair or turn into depression because our intimacy needs are no longer met. When this happens, we often tell ourselves negative things that do not serve us well.

NVC extends the meaning of mourning to include our experience at any time our needs are not met. Mourning is directly associated with a longing to get our needs met—we long to celebrate life's expression and fulfillment in our hearts.

Sometimes, celebration and mourning are closely related. While in the hospital, my dad was hungry for prayer. He wanted to connect with God, and he wanted healing to take place between us. We were able to pray together in ways we never had before. As I prayed, my face was wet with tears and my belly tight. My voice quivered, and I was overcome with emotion. This didn't happen on a street corner or in a church. It happened in the intimate space of a hospital room where it was just me, my dad, and a young pastor from Dallas named Steven.

After my dad went home to Papa Dios, I felt the deepening of our connection as bittersweet. I felt the joy of intimacy, the sadness of having to wait so long for it, and a mourning that I will have to wait until I go Home to see him again. At my father's bedside I could mourn time lost after his divorce from my mother and still celebrate his contributions to me and to others. His memorial service was very much the same, a mixture of mourning his loss and celebrating his life and his relationship to all of us.

Mourning and celebration are core needs that help us to fully acknowledge the depth of our experience. When used in conversation, they are a means to connect to God and to others. Prayer can be as simple as putting life into words and offering them up or even just sitting quietly in God's presence, listening.

Discussion

- How do you pray?
- Are there phrases you usually say when praying? Why do you say them?

- Are there topics you stay away from? Words you avoid? Why?
- How do you feel about sharing your feelings and needs in prayer?
- How comfortable are you in making requests of God?
- How do you feel when things don't work out the way you'd like? Do you blame God for the outcome?
- Have you considered that a request might be more like a demand? How do you know the difference?

31.

Transcendence and Communion

Again, I tell you that if two of you on earth agree about anything you ask for, it will be done for you by my Father in heaven. For where two or three come together in my name, there am I with them. (Matthew 18:19–20, NIV)

When I first read those verses many years ago, I was excited and asked for a new motorcycle. In fact, I even gave away my lunch money to a friend, hoping it would help; he took my money and we talked about the new motorcycle for a week. I remember daydreaming about riding through the neighborhood, waving at my friends as I rode by.

When I didn't get my motorcycle and during my rebellious teenage years, I'd point to those verses from Matthew and say things like, "See? This stuff doesn't work!" It wasn't until much later that I appreciated something closer to the message Jesus intended. He wasn't speaking about earthly material possessions, but of things much closer to the heart, in the spiritual realm.

"Peace I leave with you," he said. "My peace I give you. I do not give to you as the world gives" (John 14:27, NIV). Jesus gives to us through our hearts. Inspired by the words but uncertain of their meaning, I have pondered long on this. Here is what I think Jesus was saying to us.

The Greek word for *agree* in *if two of you on earth agree* comes from συμφωνέω or *Symphōneō*, from the same root as *symphony*. Frank Viola writes,

Symphoneo means to sound together — to be in one accord. When people achieve this sympathetic harmony, God will act. In this connection, consensus mirrors the decision-making activity within the triune God, whose nature we were created to reflect.[59]

The people involved in this conversation were willing to let go of the outcome in order to reach a mutual understanding. It is essential to interpret the conversation in the context of the whole chapter and Jesus's message in the sermon of the mount. Note that earlier in the paragraph there is a conflict.

If your brother sins against you, go and show him his fault, just between the two of you. If he listens to you, you have won your brother over. (Matthew 18:15 NIV)

I believe the meaning we can take from each phrase of this famous Bible verse is this.

Two of you on earth agree: achieving a symphony of mutual understanding through a mutual submission, a letting go of the outcome

On earth: the here and now, while we're still alive

About anything you ask for: our heart needs, our original gift of life

Will be done for you by my Father: God gave us our hearts and will meet our needs in ways we may not imagine

In heaven: you will experience something eternal, something in the spiritual realm

There am I with them: the spirit of Christ shows up in the here and now to be with us, to help us with our current situation.

Putting it all together, the message I infer from Jesus's words is this.

If we are open, simple and humble like a little child, achieving a symphony of mutual understanding, Christ's spirit comes to us, celebrating with us in our present shared experience. We get to taste living water, as the light of Christ shines within us. From this place of love beyond judgment, the Holy Spirit will help us find ways to meet our needs.

Through heartfelt empathy and honesty in our conversations, we can transcend our current situation and experience communion with Christ. By experiencing Christ in each moment, we metaphorically eat from the Tree of Life. Getting to this point is the invitation of this book. I would like to share one of these intimate moments with you now.

I got together with a few friends on a Friday night with the purpose of connecting—what we call *church*. We started off by making requests for the evening as to what we would like to do—what strategies we'd like to employ to meet some of our needs. We danced around the living room, rotating in a circle in the spirit of the Jewish tradition, listening to children's music.

This dancing had started spontaneously the last time we met, and some of us wanted to experience it again, so we danced.

Sierra, our youngest participant, was two years old. She danced in place with a shaker in each hand. The rest of us picked up tambourines, drums, triangles, and other percussion instruments and shook-rattled-drummed as we danced, one behind the next. After a couple of songs, with our hearts pounding, we collapsed onto floor pillows and couches for some connecting time. That meant having everyone in the group share how their week unfolded while the rest of us listened, sometimes offering empathy, sometimes honesty. We expressed a desire to have everyone share before 10:00 PM, when some of us start getting sleepy. We asked people to limit their sharing to five or ten minutes.

Before the sharing began, Garret, one of our music enthusiasts, played a couple of instrumental pieces and asked us to draw or express what came up for us. I felt sad and drew a cloud passing over a valley with tears falling from it into a vast, deep well. When the music ended, we went around the room and talked about our art or our week. Julie's sharing resonated with me. She spoke of pain she had felt and how her painful experience gave her a greater capacity for joy.

I was touched by what she shared. She and I talked back and forth in an almost magical experience. I felt completely understood, and so did she. I felt a deep sense of joy that brought tears to my eyes. It seemed to me that there was a kind of force field drawing us together, as if rays of light were emanating from our bodies toward each other. I find it difficult to describe it in words, and yet at the same time I feel drawn to share my experience.

To speak of authenticity, connection, intimacy, and love isn't enough; we experienced more than that. I wrote the first six lines of a poem that evening. The drawing above, along with my poem, coincided powerfully with what I was hearing Julie say. She read Kahlil Gibran's poem "On Joy and Sorrow."[60] What she shared coincided in spirit with what I had created.

Early the next morning, I completed "The Well," a poem resulting from *symphoneo,* or a symphony of mutual understanding and the feeling of Christ within us and among us.

The Well

Sweet hopeful sadness feeds the well
Which runs deep inside
Energized sadness gives me life
As I feel the pain inside me

Remembering the times which are
no more
I'm glad that I am here, and yet
drawn to what was

Never ending pain and sadness
Of what is it you speak?
Why is it that you go on living
In that pool that runs so deep?

I am grateful that there's balance
Between the sun and the rain
As it helps me to fulfill
That deep joy within the pain

It's joy I feel, needs get fulfilled
Its power gives me strength
And then in turn, I feel a burn
The well expands and fills with rain

Sadness lives again, I can't pretend
But life is bigger yet
Needs make things clear throughout
my spine
My joy and sadness do remind
Their beauty is divine

Acceptance is the one
That has done the most digging
The well is deeper now, but now filled
I find myself singing

Acceptance starts where I came from
The loving energy in my being
That made me from its flesh
Through its words

And through its seeing
'You are Good',
it said as I was coming to be
'I made you Good and filled with life,
So that you will learn I made you free'

'I made you from a love that runs so
deep
That hidden it might seem,'
'So as you find yourself just digging
As you learn, there's suffering'

'So, I made you a companion,
Someone to help you with the well
To dig it deeper
So that more joy can rest within
yourself'

'The well is filled with living water
A container you cannot hold
This living water washes all
That's covering all the gold'

'This precious metal must be shared
Or else it fades away
It must be used for bridges
For people's health and play'

'The well's a place that's built with
sadness
And great's the joy as it gets filled
With compassion and much loving
from your friends
You sing, and dance,
And then be still'

'And as you sit or lay beside
Those people who you love
Remember where you came from
And the well dug from above'

'The water that it holds
Is so precious that it sings
It brings you life and wonder,
Creation and harmony'

'So share it joyfully
With all that come around you
And feel the sadness when it comes
When some choose not to taste'

'Its fear they have inside
Its joy that's gone to waste'

'But focus on the ones
Who enjoy the sacred drink
As the tears roll off your face
They see beauty in your sadness
And the peace you help create.'

Through the intimacy of connection we can experience the eternity of Christ and the resurrection of his spirit. He sent the Counselor to be with us. We are invited to open ourselves to love and connection; the Holy Spirit does the rest.

This comes as a result of Jesus's death and resurrection, which came about so the Holy Spirit would be available to all who choose him, to help us find our way back to communion with God. Through his death, Jesus fulfilled his life purpose, becoming the Christ in his resurrection. He became an eternal being who can help us find our way back to the Garden and eat from the Tree of Life. He came so that we can all be one again. [61]

Discussion

- Sit silently, either alone or in a group. Listen.
- Describe your experience of this chapter.
- Have you ever experienced a symphony of mutual understanding? Describe it. What feelings and needs were alive in you in the moment?
- Have you ever experienced the presence of Christ? Describe how it happened.
- Have you written poetry or otherwise felt inspired to create after experiencing a moment of connection with God? If so, please share your handiwork with your friends.

IV.

COMPASSIONATE CONNECTING

Up to now we've looked at snippets and samples of NVC and how it enables us to live in harmony with our needs and values. This section goes deeper into putting NVC into practice. Most of my learning has come from completing exercises and applying the concepts in a practice group. I encourage you to find a practice group or to invite others to work through the exercises with you in a group of your own. This section is a tool to help you apply the concepts of NVC, which I extend from Marshall Rosenberg's *Nonviolent Communication: A Language of Life*. This section sets forth my experience and interpretation of NVC in light of my journey as a Christ follower, which I call Compassionate Connecting.

The picture of the Holy Family depicting Jesus, Mary and Joseph, shown on the previous page is a perfect metaphor for Compassionate Connecting—the spiritual union of love between a man and a woman brings about new life. This metaphor beautifully extends to the union of the two sides of connection—empathy (female) and honesty (male) that brings about the new life of Christ, as we explored in the previous chapter (Matthew 18:19-20). The first chapter of the gospel according to John echoes the two sides of connection: *grace and truth came through Jesus Christ* — empathy is a form of grace and honesty is a form of truth.

Compassionate Connecting is also like dancing. As we listen to the music of each other's hearts and we begin to co-create our own tunes, a new sound emerges in harmony and in sync. We move together in time and space, taking turns expressing new desires and directions for our journey. As we get to know the other, we gain a new perspective of ourselves in relation to the other. We gain a new freedom to move about that celebrates both our own contribution to the mix and the creative expression of the other. We discover that there is enough air and space for still others to join our dance, and we long for all to share in the celebration of life—a gift of love from God.

32.

Relational Framework

This section provides a conceptual framework for the practice of NVC and a further discussion of the words it uses, such as *heart, mind, body, soul,* and *spirit* – which are used throughout the Bible as foundational elements of love in Deuteronomy 6:4-9, Leviticus 19:18, Mark 12:30-31, Matt 22:36-40, and Luke 10:27. The gospel of John further cements the role of love in following the Way of Christ:

> *This is how everyone will recognize that you are my disciples – when they see the love you have for each other.* (John 13:35, Message)

This study and the exercises that accompany it have enabled me to integrate these concepts with the words and events of everyday life. It supports my particular learning style. My interpretation is offered as a way to help you understand NVC and use it successfully within the Judeo-Christian context as a means to loving connection with God, each other and ourselves – not as a means to theological proofs.

Understanding, clarity, and integration are the needs addressed in this chapter; its purpose is to demonstrate how OFNR fits into existing frameworks. This is particularly helpful in interpreting the Bible, for it uses the words listed above without formally defining them in relation to each other.

In the first chapter of *The Powers that Be: Theology for a New Millennium,* Walter Wink describes worldviews that define how we think and view our surroundings.

In the *Ancient Worldview,* heaven and earth are clearly separated. Everything earthly (events as well as matter) has a heavenly counterpart and vice versa.

In the *Spiritualist Worldview*, heaven is spiritual and good and everything earthly, such as matter, is evil.

The *Materialist Worldview* is the opposite of the Spiritualist Worldview. Everything spiritual is rejected: there is no heaven, no spirit, no God. The material world is all that exists.

The *Theological Worldview* values a separated heaven and earth where all things spiritual are in heaven and all things earthly are conceded to science.

The *Integral Worldview* sees everything as having an inner and outer aspect, where heaven and earth are different aspects of a single reality. Spiritual and physical attributes are perspectives of our life experience.

The Integral Worldview is the most consistent with my experience and understanding. Through this view, we see the stories in the Bible as part of our current experience. For example, as we make a moral judgment, we metaphorically eat from the Tree of Knowledge of Good and Evil—the Tree of Judgment. Judgment is the plank that keeps us from seeing clearly, and self-empathy is a way to remove the plank. Empathy is the way to help others deal with their specks, and honesty is a way to see the truth that will set me free.

The Integral Worldview supports my communicating in accordance with my values, where my inner world is in harmony with my actions. I am doing my best to live the gospel message as opposed to just studying it, talking about it, or pushing it on someone else. I try not to be like the hypocrite Pharisees and scribes, but attempt to be more like Jesus and live in integrity.

In *Things Hidden: Scripture as Spirituality*, Richard Rohr describes a cosmic egg made up of layers, or *domes*, of meaning, like the nested matryoshka dolls of Russia.

In the outer dome, Rohr says, is The Story of the really big picture, the truth of what is. These are the things that are always true, which we try to infer from our experience and inherited wisdom.

In the next dome is Our Story, which defines the communal group identities and loyalties that expand our sense of self, such as ethnicity, groupthink, nationalism, and cultural religion. He points out that conservatives and more traditional people tend to value this dome more than others. This dome represents our collective story, which tries to preserve our shared wisdom from generation to generation. New ideas are feared because of the desire to preserve the valued wisdom of our ancestors. The Bible can be seen as a collection of shared wisdom preserved through the ages—how groups of people interpret it is symbolized by this dome.

In the innermost dome, Rohr defines My Story, or the private experience of the individual. He says that many liberals value this dome more than others. Here each person is focused on the inner world of personal experience, often as a result of earlier pain, that can stimulate a desire for health, growth, and living a full life.

The framework I will present is an extension of all these stories and worldviews. I propose another dome of meaning: a Relational Story where individuals share their own stories with others, through honest expression. The other person listens and connects with the speaker, giving empathy. Many of the characters in the Bible, particularly Jesus, were inviting us into the Relational Story.

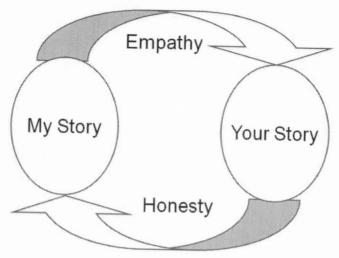

Figure 4. Relational Story Dome

After the first story is told, the participants switch roles. The Relational Story dome differs from the Our Story dome in that the relational experiences are uniquely individual and dynamically changing based on the participant's experiences of the moment. The Our Story dome is made up of accepted beliefs, static identifications, and assumptions.

This new Relational Story dome is similar to Walter Wink's Integral Worldview. Through empathy and honesty, we expand our sense of who we are, discovering the similarities between people. We experience our universal connection through our common source. The deeper the connection between people, the more integrated are our spiritual and material worlds—our heavenly and earthly worlds are joined.

Extending the metaphor of the matryoshka dolls, the third dome would not contain a single doll but rather a multiplicity of them that physically touch each other in one spot but are separated everywhere else. The place where they touch symbolizes their connection, and the space in between symbolizes each person's autonomy and freedom of experience.

The Our Story dome is still applicable; it symbolizes the things we take for granted as labels, prejudices, and cultural conditioning. This dome shows up in My Story as the things that I tell myself. As we learn to identify these and move beyond them by separating observations from evaluations, we can gain some freedom from the Our Story container—the dome gets thinner.

The nature of The Story changes as we share in the Relational Story. Our mutual understanding, acceptance, and connection transcend intellectual understanding, and we reach the possibility of intimacy and oneness with each other. Here our needs for acceptance, belonging, peace, harmony, beauty, mutuality, and love are met. Getting to the point of connection and its mystery is the invitation of this book and the invitation of Christ to love one another.

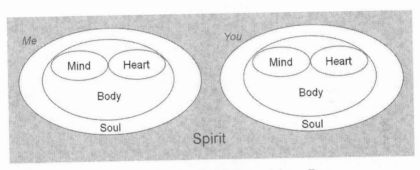

Figure 5. Static Model of Relational Story Dome

In Figure 5 above, the Relational Story domes are shown as You and Me ovals. Each oval is made up of a soul and a physical body containing the heart and mind. The soul encompasses the ethereal self that remains after the body dies. The word *heart* is used as a symbol of what is real and true for us, the part of us that contains our needs and values. The word *mind* is used as a symbol for our information processing and decision making.

Our focus will be on the interactions between the heart and mind as we shine the light of consciousness on the dynamics of communication using OFNR. A further level of framing will show how OFNR relates to the concepts defined so far.

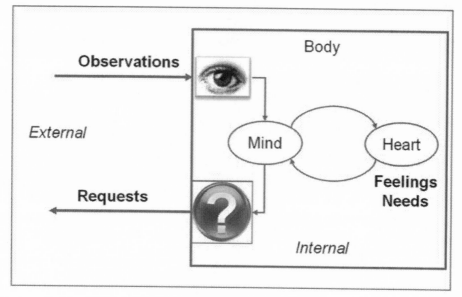

Figure 6. Body Context Diagram

The diagram in Figure 6 shows the objects of interest in relation to their environment. The body is the main object, since it contains the heart and mind. There are things external to the body and things internal to it. A person, with their body, interacts with the external world through observations and requests; the rest of the dialogue is internal. The mind acts as a gateway between the external world and the internal world. Not only does it route information by enabling our consciousness to perceive the maelstrom of the world, but it also evaluates the information it receives. When information comes in, a foundational decision is made.

Do I make a value judgment to see if needs are met or do I make a moral judgment of good or bad?

In the case of a value judgment, the mind is focused internally; in the case of a moral judgment, the mind is focused externally. This is the point at which we get to re-live and participate in the creation story—we make a choice on whether to eat from the Tree of Judgment or the Tree of Life. One choice leads to violence, the other leads to love. Attention follows our choice of our source of reference: the mind's perception of truth. The framework in which the mind evaluates things is extremely important and will be discussed in more detail later. For now, we will limit ourselves to its role of shifting our awareness from one place to another.

Observation is typically associated with eyesight, but here we generalize to our experience of the world through all five senses and the thinking that takes place afterward. As we observe and experience the world, feelings are stimulated. They tell us if our needs are being met, and if so, our feelings are pleasant. We experience unpleasant feelings when our needs are not met. When the mind is clear on our internal experience through self-empathy, we are self-connected. We might feel lightness, compassion, and curiosity toward others.

A natural result of self-empathy is a feeling of peace, a sense of harmony and integration in which the heart and mind are no longer separate entities. When we focus the mind externally— before taking care of our *plank*—instead of internally, we often experience blame and moral judgment toward others, and the heart and mind remain separate and disconnected from each other. On the other hand, after removing our plank through self-empathy, we have more clarity and freedom to interact with the world in ways consistent with our values because our minds are connected with our hearts.

Needs words are at the core of our life experience, as they point to what we require and value about life. Needs are at the heart of the gift of life that we received at creation. Everyone has the same needs, but different needs are active at different times. A need word describes life energy seeking fulfillment of the heart. Given that we require words to communicate, we are limited to using the mind to describe heart things. When focusing on needs, what is really important is to transcend the mind's label and connect with the experience that the word signifies.

For example, when I think of my need for beauty, I often transport myself to the time I first came upon a sunset over the Pacific Ocean in Southern California. There were shades of red, orange, yellow, green, blue, purple, mixed white puffy clouds that contrasted with the changing depths of blue ocean. I felt a sense of awe. There's a lot behind the word *beauty*, and people may differ in their definitions of the word, but we can rest in the knowledge that a loving God placed this in our hearts. That we can find something in common with others given the love we infer from the experience of beauty in spite of our different definitions.

As we become aware of our feelings and needs, we may choose to make requests of others, of God, and of ourselves. Without requests, other people don't know what we want. People can be confused when requests are not made. Requests are the means by which our internal world speaks with the external world. Requests are not always verbalized; sometimes we just act when we make a request to ourselves—if we're hungry, we eat; we breathe without much thought. Verbalized requests become much more important when other people are involved. Conflict can result from verbalizing our requests as demands or from not verbalizing them clearly or at all.

As we engage others in conversation using empathy and honesty, and we begin to connect, the Relational Story dome begins to integrate. I try to show this integration in the dynamic model of Figure 7. The apparent separateness and duality of the heart and mind go away as we learn to relax into the cycle of life. We move between our heart needs and our mind strategies as we consciously participate in life. The interaction between the heart and the mind is our way of forming a creative union with God.

The left side of Figure 7 shows the hearts and minds of two people coming together in intimacy. The minds combine into one, and the hearts merge into one. As this happens, the minds are no longer minds, and the hearts no longer hearts—they become something new. As we remain in intimacy, sometimes God offers us a little more. The lightning bolt symbolizes the transition to communion, not by our effort, but by a gift of the Holy Spirit. In communion we are whole and integrated. The circle on the right is another representation of Wink's Integral View. As we move from a static model showing a separation of heart, mind, body, and soul, to a dynamic model supporting communion and integration, we see a movement from the Theological to the Integral Worldview, a movement from intellectual belief toward an integrated way of life. This symbol of communion can also be seen as a metaphor for integrity, where we line up our collective inner and outer selves, and we become self-similar and integrated. We are no longer alone; we are home.

I love the symmetry in the dynamic model, especially the right half. It reminds me of the mystical Body of Christ that we celebrate in Holy Communion, when we eat from the bread of life and taste the fruit of the Kingdom picked from the Tree of Life. We can get to this stage by accepting the invitation to the banquet—through the grace of empathy and the honest expression of our truth—exemplified by the life, death, and resurrection of Christ.

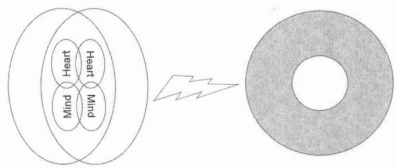

Figure 7. Dynamic Model of Relational Story Dome: Intimacy and Communion

The remainder of this section will show how the concepts discussed here can be put into practice through Compassionate Connecting.

33.

Awareness: Observation vs. Evaluation

Have you ever stated what you thought was a fact and had it interpreted differently by the other person? If the conversation took an unexpected turn, you might have included some evaluation in your statement. The other person heard something you didn't intend. The problem with evaluations is that they're open to interpretation. A speaker will intend to say one thing, and the other person hears something else, breaking connection, or at least causing confusion.

Webster's online dictionary says that observation is "The act of making and recording a measurement and The act of noticing or paying attention."[62] The video camera analogy applies to what you want to state as fact: If you can't see it through the lens, you might be evaluating instead of observing.

An evaluation determines the value, quality, or significance of something. It adds subjective experience to what is being said, usually in the form of a label. Evaluations and judgments limit the ability to maintain a connection because the other person's interpretation interferes. To connect, start with observations, not evaluations.

Some evaluations are more difficult to identify than others. For example, *I experience you as* _____ is an evaluation that takes responsibility for the internal stimulus but does not contribute to connection. It is an expression of mind analysis, not feelings or needs.

Exercise

Circle the numbers of the statements that contain observations. If an evaluation is identified, craft a related sentence as an observation.

1. All she does is complain.
2. He said that he gets angry when he sees violence on TV.
3. Your music is too loud.
4. Sam is aggressive.
5. Peter yelled at me when I walked in the door.
6. I was waiting my turn, and he cut in line.
7. She showed no regard for me.
8. Sandy walked away after I expressed my disappointment.
9. My son often forgets to brush his teeth.
10. Ellen works too much.
11. Jaime said that he didn't like his gift.
12. I experience you as a great speaker.

Responses

1. *Evaluation.* The word *complain* is labeling her actions and doesn't describe what she said. An observation might be, "The last two times we talked, she said she was tired of her job."

2. *Observation.* The speaker is quoting someone else's remark about getting angry when he sees violence on TV.

3. *Evaluation. Too loud* is open to interpretation. Describing audio levels is challenging to express as an observation.

An observation might sound like it came from an engineering textbook: "The average sound pressure level of your sound system is 99 decibels measured at 1 foot from your speakers." Given that most people don't have the kind of equipment to make this observation on hand, you might say, "I'm noticing that the dishes are shaking," or "I can feel the sound of the bass reverberating through the floor."

4. *Evaluation. Aggressive* has many different meanings. An observation here might be, "The last time Sam spoke to me, his face was within a foot of mine" or "Sam had the team's highest sales numbers for two months in a row."

5. *Evaluation. Yelled at me* seems to imply that Peter is doing something wrong. Something closer to an observation would be, "As soon as I walked in the door, Peter said that he was really unhappy with my work."

6. *Evaluation. He cut in line* seems to imply that an injustice was committed. Something closer to an observation might be, "When I arrived at the line to get on the ski lift, I noticed that he arrived after me; after five minutes of waiting in line, I noticed he was in front of me."

7. *Evaluation. Showed no regard* doesn't describe what she did. An observation for this sentiment might be, "I arrived at her home and she didn't say a word" or "I said 'excuse me,' but her expression didn't change."

8. *Evaluation. Expressed my disappointment* means different things to different people. An observation would be, "Sandy walked away after I told her I was disappointed."

9. *Evaluation. Often forgets* is subject to interpretation. An observation in this instance might be, "I didn't see my son brushing his teeth after we arrived home from the party last night."

10. *Evaluation. Works too much* is subject to interpretation. An observation might be, "I noticed that Ellen arrived home

after 8:00 PM every night this week" or "Ellen's timecard had over fifty hours a week for the last two months."

11. *Observation.* "This is a quote of something that Jaime said."

12. *Evaluation. Great speaker* is an evaluation. I could incorporate an observation into my honesty—the observation part: "Your speech only lasted five minutes." The honesty: "I was touched by your speech as it met my needs for hope."

Discussion

- Do you find yourself making evaluations in casual conversation? What do they sound like?
- Did you find it difficult to make observations?
- Do you find you're judging yourself as a result of this exercise? What are you telling yourself?

34.

Experience: Feelings vs. Thoughts

I am often surprised at the interpretations of feelings that I hear from my friends, as if having unpleasant feelings is bad. Among some people, it's as if the happy face is the only acceptable one. I feel frustrated and sad when I interact with them because I want more authenticity and honesty regarding feelings. I like the freedom to feel whatever is going on inside me and to choose whether or not to express it.

Feelings are neither good nor bad, they just tell us if our needs are being met or not. Feelings are a message from our inner being, our heart, that say it is somehow being stimulated by something going on either inside or outside of us.

Our feelings are often confused with our thoughts. Thoughts are the result of analysis or evaluation, a comparison or judgment. They can masquerade as feelings, especially when we use the word *feel* or *feeling* as we often do. For example, if I say, "I feel like I was hit by a large truck," a thought is expressed, not a feeling. But if I say, "I feel tired and overwhelmed and want to go home," feelings are expressed.

There is a way of expressing feelings that looks outside of us for the *cause* of our experience, instead of acknowledging the actions of others as a *stimulus*. Outside events have an effect on us, but they don't cause feelings. To say "*I feel sad because you left*" gives the power of responsibility away and can be a strategy intended to induce guilt in the other person—this has also been described as a *victim strategy*. In the chapter on needs, we explore how needs help us to take responsibility for our experience by acknowledging our own truth.

Here are a couple of short lists of feelings—a reference list of common feelings and needs appears at the end of this book. A helpful strategy for learning feelings and needs is to put the list on the refrigerator and look at it daily and identify the feelings and needs alive in you. Make it fun: use different colored pencils to underline or circle the words that describe your experiences of the day. For longer lists of feelings and needs, go to the Center for Nonviolent Communication at www.cnvc.org.

➢ Happy	➢ Delighted	➢ Relieved	➢ Pleased
➢ Joyful	➢ Inspired	➢ Peaceful	➢ Comfortable
➢ Grateful	➢ Amazed	➢ Centered	➢ Satisfied
➢ Touched	➢ Enchanted	➢ Relaxed	➢ Alive
➢ Hopeful	➢ Compassion	➢ Content	➢ Passionate
➢ Excited			

Figure 8. Feelings Stimulated When Needs Are Met

➢ Sad	➢ Depressed	➢ Jealous	➢ Guilty
➢ Afraid	➢ Cranky	➢ Unhappy	➢ Ashamed
➢ Anxious	➢ Annoyed	➢ Bored	➢ Torn
➢ Upset	➢ Resentful	➢ Lonely	➢ Suspicious
➢ Worried	➢ Angry	➢ Disappointed	➢ Vulnerable
➢ Hurt	➢ Confused	➢ Discouraged	➢ Frustrated
➢ Embarrassed	➢ Tired	➢ Longing	➢ Irritated

Figure 9. Feelings Stimulated When Needs Are Not Met

As a general rule, if the words *like* or *that* follow *feel* or *feeling*, it's likely that a thought, not a feeling, is being expressed. This exercise is designed to show the difference between the two.

Exercise

Circle the number if a feeling is expressed in the sentences below. If not, construct a sentence for that situation that expresses a feeling.

1. I feel like going to the gym.
2. I'm sad that you didn't show up in time for dinner.
3. I feel manipulated when you walk away.
4. I'm pleased with our conversation, even though we disagree.
5. You piss me off when you don't ask me first.
6. I'm anxious because I'd like more safety.
7. I feel good when it's sunny outside.
8. I'm frustrated because I want to use my time efficiently.
9. You irritate me when you leave your dirty clothes on the floor.
10. I'm losing patience with you.

Responses to Exercise

1. No. The phrase *feel like going to the gym* doesn't express a feeling. Expressing a feeling could be, "I'm excited to go to the gym, as I enjoy its health benefits—better rest, leaner body, more aliveness."
2. Yes. Sadness is a feeling.
3. No. *Manipulated* is an evaluative word implying that someone else is causing (as opposed to stimulating) a feeling in us. Expressing a feeling in this instance might be, "I feel annoyed when you walk away because my needs for respect aren't met, and I'd like you to value my needs as much as yours."
4. Yes. Being pleased is a feeling.

5. *Pisses me off* is slang for anger, which is a feeling. More clearly, I might say, "I'm angry because I want more consideration—I want to feel that we both matter."

6. Yes. Anxiety is a feeling.

7. The word *good* is more of an evaluation than a feeling. At the same time, it does imply that the feelings are pleasant as opposed to unpleasant and that needs are being met. Using a word more specific than *good* can bring about a greater connection. The specific word might be *happy, grateful, delighted* or any of the feeling words. "When it's sunny, I'm inspired to go outside and play with my friends."

8. Yes. *Frustration* is a feeling that is stimulated when needs aren't being met.

9. Yes. A feeling of irritation is being expressed, but the other person is made out to be the cause, not the stimulus. "When I see your clothes on the floor, I feel irritated because I value order and beauty."

10. No. A feeling is not being expressed when I lose patience. The feeling behind it might be *annoyance, resentment,* or *impatience.* It could sound like, "I see that we've been talking for forty-five minutes. I'm feeling frustrated because I want more clarity, and I need some rest."

Discussion

- How often in daily conversation do you use feelings to describe your inner experience?

- How often do you use thought language to describe your inner experience?

- Do you ever confuse feelings with thoughts? When?

- What is the cost of confusing feelings with thoughts?

- What is the benefit of using feelings in dialogue?

35.

Motivation: Needs vs. Strategies

Build up others according to their needs. (Ephesians 4:29, NIV)

Visualizing the beauty of our needs to see past the words we use to describe them enhances our chances of connecting with others. Heart needs are at the core of our existence and acknowledging them helps us take responsibility for our experience. Needs are like the musical instruments of our lives; each one may be active, silent or playing with other instruments — they enable God's melody of love to bring life to us. Needs are hard to put into exact definitions because they come from the heart, and seem to have a life of their own. My favorite definition of need is *life energy in us seeking fulfillment.*

The kingdom of God is within you. (Luke 17:21, NIV)

Needs come from God. They are a gift to us, and acknowledging them is a celebration of the gift of life. It's a form of worship of the Creator as one feels a deep gratitude for everything that is. Creation itself came out of the love of God for us—he created the universe so that love could be manifested through the conversation of life.

Acknowledging our needs is essential to being present to ourselves and others, for they connect us with what is true for us in the moment. As we share our needs with others in conversation, we may choose to celebrate our divine connection with God as we experience connection with another person.

Strategies, on the other hand, are actions, people, places, or things we select to meet a need. We require strategies to live. We must have shelter—preferably a home. We must breathe, eat, and drink. The heart calls us to connect and to love each other. We should stay connected to our needs as much as possible, but we must identify strategies and make requests in order to get our needs met.

The following illustration in Figure 10 shows this cycle of life. It is a two-state diagram, where the ovals indicate the states and the arrows show the transitions between them. As our awareness is focused on our needs, we can imagine the Needs oval lit up while the other oval remains dark. Once we formulate a request to get the need met, we turn to the Strategy oval and see it light up while the Needs oval darkens. We experience freedom when we can let go of the strategy and return to our needs, shown in the transition between the two ovals and labeled Letting Go of the Outcome.

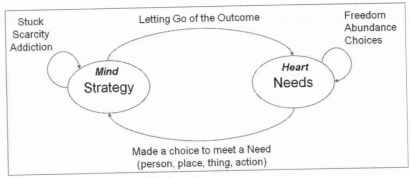

Figure 10. Life-Cycle Diagram

A problem arises when we become attached to a specific strategy. In the extreme, such an attachment is often labeled *addiction*. There was a time when I tried to get all my connection needs met by my significant other. At another time, I dealt with stress by smoking cigarettes. There was a long period in my life when I identified myself solely as an electrical engineer. This identification with strategy is often called *ego identification*.[63] As we let go of our ego's chosen strategies and solutions, we metaphorically die on the cross, and might feel sadness, anxiety or grief.

We experience joy when we live in a flow between needs and strategies and don't get stuck in either state; getting stuck leads to the unpleasant feelings, such as sadness, anxiety, and frustration. In the diagram, needs are associated with the heart and strategies with the mind. As we allow ourselves to flow freely between the heart and the mind, we begin to experience harmony, integration, and fullness and even other pleasant feelings, such as joy, happiness, contentment, and gratitude.

Strategies are necessary, but we experience more joy by connecting with the life energy of needs and rediscovering the original gift of life that is within us—the gift that comes directly from our creator God, the source of all life.

It is important not to confuse the need words with their meaning and the love behind them. The words themselves are a reminder of the love of God, which is difficult to describe with words. Imagination, an important element of connecting to needs, helps us to transcend language and hear the message of love. Needs words are a reminder of God's desire that we experience love through the life we've been given. Sometimes poetry or music comes closer to reminding us of the gift of life than needs words do.

I have had several experiences of deep connection with God in the wilderness. When I went backpacking with a friend I had what I call a God moment—an experience of beauty, peace and communion with God. I was surrounded by hundreds of shades of green in a meadow that few people had ever seen. In that meadow, I experienced God asking me to invite others into communion, to live and taste the beauty of creation. In answer to him, I wrote the following poem.

Out to the Mountains

I went out to the mountains
To get away from it all
The noise, the clutter,
The hustle and bustle
And found some reprieve
In nature's soft tussle

I went there for rest
And a little adventure
And maybe connection
With the creator of nature

It's communion I seek
With such divine love
Which inspire me so
I leave comfort and home

My eyes do get misty
As my belly contracts
As I packed on the trail
And headed my way back

I stood on a hill
And looked back to the meadow

Which brought me such joy
And yet I'm unsettled

The beauty enveloped
My soul in a way
That I felt a deep joy
And yet sadness that day

How could it have been
That this place was created?
What was in the heart
Of this being that made it?

And what is inside me
That longs for this sight
Which brings me to travel
So far through the night?

What words could I use
To describe such a moment?
When the sun rises up
And wakes up all that's living?

My soul wants to sing
And it's just the beginning

The diagram in Figure 11 by Jim and Jori Manske[64] organizes needs geometrically. The physical needs, such as survival, food, and shelter, are at the bottom. The personal or individual needs, such as autonomy, meaning, and honesty, are on the left. The interpersonal needs, such as protection, justice, support, community, and empathy, are on the right. The transcendent or spiritual needs, such as beauty, harmony, and space, are on top.

209

Figure 11. Needs Diagram

Exercise

Determine whether a need is being expressed in each sentence. If not, what do you think the unspoken need is?

1. I need coffee to help me wake up.
2. I enjoy the beauty of the mountains.
3. I'm disappointed you couldn't make it; I was hoping to spend time with you.
4. I enjoyed the birthday party celebration.
5. I feel anxious when you yell at me.
6. I'm concerned with emailing my intellectual property.
7. Others say things that hurt me.
8. I'm annoyed that you're late.
9. I'm grateful for your help, because I wanted to finish before the game.

Responses to Exercise

1. Coffee is not a need. The need could be for aliveness or clarity.
2. Beauty is considered a need that helps one live more fully, perhaps celebrating the appreciation of creation.
3. *Spend time with you* implies a need for connection, companionship.
4. The word *celebration* expresses a need.
5. No need is expressed. The needs could be for respect, consideration, peace, harmony, or mutuality.
6. No need is expressed. The needs could be for protection, privacy, financial support, or safety.
7. No need is expressed. The needs could be for self-protection, trust, self-connection, empathy, or consideration.

8. No need is expressed. The needs could be for respect for time, efficiency, consideration, or connection.

9. *Finish before the game* implies a need for efficient use of time, but it does not express it directly.

Discussion

- What comes up for you when you hear the word *need?*

- In some communities, the word *need* has a negative connotation, as in, "Don't be so needy." Why do you think this is the case?

36.

Action: Requests vs. Demands

Ask and it will be given to you. (Matthew 7:7, NIV)

This chapter highlights the dynamics of asking for what we want—formulating a strategy for getting our needs met. The asking could take the form of a request or a demand. I have noticed that most conversations traditionally start with some sort of a request/demand. In NVC, we are invited to consider including observations, feelings and needs before a request, making it more likely that we will stay connected. Without heart information, requests however well-intentioned, will usually be interpreted as demands—when *no* is not acceptable.

Another important element of requests is clarity—we must verbalize what is being requested to be done and when. I used to have a wish that I'm guessing a lot of us have: *I want you to know what I want without my having to ask for it.* I probably developed this wish before I could even talk, but it lived on past its useful lifetime. I was surprised and frustrated to hear the same expectation from my ex-wife near the end of our marriage. I now feel some sadness and regret that back then I didn't have the skills I have now to support the kind of connection I wanted and especially that we didn't have more clarity between us. We struggled to verbalize what we wanted. When I made a request, I was afraid she would say no and pull away from me emotionally.

I'm guessing that many of my requests back in what I call my age of scarcity sounded like demands, because inside my heart they were demands. I was not okay if my strategies weren't followed with complete compliance. I would retaliate in an attempt to make the other person pay for my pain and disappointment. I acted passive-aggressively: I disappeared emotionally from the relationship or did things I knew would upset the other person as punishment. There were times when I would dump my feelings onto someone so that they would feel guilty or ashamed and move closer to doing what I wanted. I would make my requests vague in the hope that the other person would take a risk and make the definitive request for me. For example, say I just arrived from work after a long day and I'm hungry. Instead of expressing my full honesty ending with a request, I'd say something like, "I'm starving" and nothing else, expecting my wife to offer to cook something to eat. At least for a while, she would respond with, "Would you like me to prepare dinner for you?"

The full honesty of what I said might sound like, "Honey, I'm starving; would you be willing to prepare something for dinner?" or "I'm guessing you're as tired as I am hungry — would you like to go out for dinner tonight?"

The tragedy was that over time, when my partner would actually do what I requested, it was sometimes from fear of punishment, not from a place of joy, self-connection, and wanting to contribute to my well-being. This form of expectations, or *mind reading*, can make long-term committed relationships difficult to maintain.

Today, making requests is an empowering way I can express the truth of what would be wonderful for me and bring completion to my part of the dialogue. Sometimes I still experience some discomfort at giving my honesty and making a request from people I'm close to, fearing that they'll leave. But just knowing this brings about a self-compassion that empowers me to ask for what I want. These days, as I experience the abundance of life and the many ways needs can be met, I recover quickly when I'm told no.

I encourage my family and friends to be honest with me and to give to me only if it meets their own needs. I'm much more careful in accepting gifts from people who are acting out of duty, obligation, guilt, or shame, or who want to buy love. I've learned from experience that receiving gifts from that kind of heart will lead to disharmony, conflict or even violence. Dr. Rosenberg often says that someone's going to pay when giving under duress.

A friend recently asked me to help her at a fund-raising event. When I said that I couldn't help because I was finishing a draft of this book on deadline, this was her response.

> *In the year that I've known you, I've never asked you to do anything. I'm a really busy person; I'm constantly organizing events. Last time you asked for help reviewing a draft, I stayed up until 4:00 AM working on it, and now that I need help, you're unwilling to give it.*

This sounded to me like a demand. I interpreted her words as an attempt to make me feel guilty so that I would meet her need for support. I heard that my friend was overwhelmed, but when she brought up the times she helped me, I could see that the help wasn't freely given; there were strings attached. At this point I became concerned about accepting help from her because I thought she would try to make me pay for it later.

I was torn about helping my friend with her event. I want to support her but I also needed autonomy and self-respect. I became wary of meeting her need for support at the expense of my own desire to contribute through my book. The joy of doing so was gone—I could not support her with integrity, so I said no.

Demands are costly in a relationship, while requests that the other person is free to refuse are more likely to deepen the connection in the long run because it fosters trust in that both sides are being honest. Requests in which both sides are free to refuse and accept also make life more enjoyable when the answer comes back in the affirmative—there's safety in knowing that a price won't be paid now or later, maximizing the enjoyment in fulfilling the request.

Before making requests for the strategies you have in mind, it is important to have a connection resulting from several rounds of OFNR. Here are three common requests that are helpful in connecting with others in conversation.

1. Would you be willing to tell me what you heard me say?

This is usually the first type of request to be made when giving honesty, not only to make sure the other person heard and understood the message, but also because it's important they aren't hearing judgment, criticism or a demand. If they are, it will usually come out in their reply. This question is also a way to request empathy from the other person: another form of the question is, "Would you be willing to empathize with what I just said?"

2. How do you feel when you hear me say this?

This question is especially helpful to invite a transition in the conversation after we're understood. It gives the other person a chance to express themselves through their own honesty, effectively signaling that it's now your turn to speak about yourself. The roles then switch: the person previously giving honesty now gives empathy and vice versa. After a few rounds of role-switching, the connection begins to deepen, and it will be more fruitful to consider strategies and specific actions.

3. Would you be willing to explore some strategies?

This third question signals the final stage of a conversation thread. All three questions listed are present-time requests. If the next request is for something to happen in the future, it helps to be clear exactly when it will happen; otherwise, the other person doesn't know what's expected, and the two of you might disconnect later.

It's important to have a heart connection before exploring strategies. This will release the Holy Spirit to work for us, for we are now open to hearing the Spirit. A brainstorm of solutions at this point can produce mutually satisfying strategies that will meet everyone's needs.

I'm constantly amazed at the power of clear and doable requests. They put words to our desires and help us let go of the outcome. Making requests is empowering because it completes our need for honest expression and makes it more likely that our needs will be met.

The more we experience the abundance of needs, the more relaxed we feel when we make requests and the more easily we can accept whatever answers are given. We have the freedom to choose to meet our needs by other strategies if the person says no. Hearing *no* can help us discover what's alive in the other person, but it can also be the end of the conversation.

The important part is that we are willing to hear the other person as we strive not only to be true to ourselves, but also to show respect to the other. We are seeking a symphony of the heart that comes to life with mutual understanding, regardless of the answer to the request—the *symphoneo* described in Matthew 18:19–20.

Exercise

Are these sentences clear and doable requests? If not, what request might be applicable to the situation?

1. Would you help me create a peaceful environment?
2. Please understand me.

3. Would you like to go out?

4. Would you be willing to be here before 7:00 PM tonight?

5. I'd like you to love me more.

6. Would you please respect me?

7. I want you to stop smoking.

8. Let's go to an AA meeting on Saturday at 7:00 AM.

9. I want you to be happy.

10. Tell me one thing you like about your job.

11. I want you to keep your room clean.

Responses

1. It is not clear what is being requested. "How exactly would you like me to help create a peaceful environment?" would be an appropriate follow-up question. A clear and doable request might be, "Would you be willing to go with me to an NVC workshop this Saturday from 1:00 to 4:00 PM?"

2. It is not clear what is being requested. A clear and doable request to help with my need for understanding might be, "Would you be willing to listen to me for the next fifteen minutes while I try to explain my position?" and "Would you be willing to tell me what you heard me say?"

3. It isn't clear what is being requested. A clear and doable request might be, "I'm going to the movies tomorrow in Irvine at 7:00 PM to see *The Matrix* again. Would you like to join me?" or "Would you like to go out for coffee tomorrow? I know a great coffee shop in Laguna; I could meet you there at 1:30."

4. This is a clear and doable request.

5. It isn't clear what is being requested here; love means different things to different people. A clear and doable request might be, "Would you be willing to cook a five-course dinner and do the dishes tonight?" or "My back

is sore; would you be willing to give me a thirty-minute massage?"

6. It isn't clear what is being requested here, as the need for respect can be met in different ways. A clear and doable request might be "Next time I enter the room, would you be willing to say hello to me?"

7. It isn't clear what is being requested. *Stop smoking* is asking the person to stop doing something instead of asking for something to be done. A clear and doable request might be, "Would you consider going to the doctor tomorrow morning at 7:00 AM to talk about ways to help you quit smoking?"

8. This is a clear and doable request.

9. What is being requested? It's hard to imagine a clear and doable request for someone else's happiness. Perhaps the following question gets closer: "Is there something I might be able to do to help you?"

10. This is a clear and doable request.

11. *Keep your room clean* is not clear and doable. One person's "clean" is unlikely to be the same as the other person's. A clear and doable request might be, "Would you be willing to pick your clothes up off the floor, hang them up in the closet, and vacuum the carpet by 5:00 PM today?"

Discussion

- Have you ever made a vague request? How did it turn out for you?

- Have you had the experience of someone telling you how they feel but not telling you what they want from you? How did you feel?

- Is it difficult for you to make requests of others? Why or why not?

37.

Freeing the Victim: Evaluative Words Can Sound Like Feelings

Some strategies to get our needs met have an implied demand attached to them. When we don't take responsibility for our feelings and needs, we might blame or project, seeing another person as the source of our discomfort instead of as a stimulus. They may be triggering an experience from the past, and we react by reliving those feelings and thoughts. This is commonly called a *Victim Strategy.*

The good news is that victim strategies can be identified by evaluative words that sound like feelings but are more like evaluations of the other person's behavior. These common words are at the core of avoiding responsibility for our feelings and needs. This strategy implies that someone else is responsible for them—that someone is causing our feelings.

In NVC, personal responsibility for feelings and needs is extremely important. In NVC we acknowledge responsibility for listening to our feelings as part of our uniquely personal experience of getting our needs met. We don't blame others for our feelings. We differentiate between cause and stimulus.

The stimulus is the event occurring right now. Excluding physical violence, the cause of a feeling is often an interpretation of something that happened a long time ago that we're comparing to something happening now. Many commonly used evaluative words are shown below; for a more complete list with translations, go to http://en.nvcwiki.com/index.php/Evaluative_words.

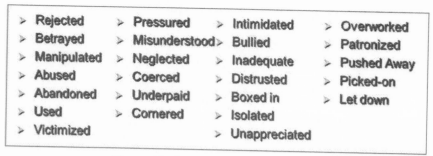

➤ Rejected	➤ Pressured	➤ Intimidated	➤ Overworked
➤ Betrayed	➤ Misunderstood	➤ Bullied	➤ Patronized
➤ Manipulated	➤ Neglected	➤ Inadequate	➤ Pushed Away
➤ Abused	➤ Coerced	➤ Distrusted	➤ Picked-on
➤ Abandoned	➤ Underpaid	➤ Boxed in	➤ Let down
➤ Used	➤ Cornered	➤ Isolated	
➤ Victimized		➤ Unappreciated	

Figure 12. Common Evaluative Words

When we hear ourselves or others use these words, we might give empathy to determine what feelings and needs are behind them. For example, I might say, "My girlfriend broke up with me and rejected me — on the phone!"

The phrase *broke up* is an evaluation, and the word *rejected* is an evaluative word. Using self-empathy, I might translate the sentence into something like this.

My girlfriend called me yesterday and said, "I'm breaking up with you." I'm feeling sad because I miss our connection and intimacy. I'm also annoyed because I want more consideration — that she value my needs as much as hers. I would have preferred that she tell me in person.

"My girlfriend called me yesterday and said 'I'm breaking up with you'" is the observation. After saying that, I explore the feelings and needs present. My feelings are stated as, "I'm feeling sad because I miss our connection and intimacy."

Relationships tend to stimulate lots of feelings, particularly when they end. So, we could expect many different feelings and needs to describe our experience. In this case, another feeling is, "I'm annoyed because I want more consideration — I would have preferred that she tell me in person."

People who use evaluative words in place of feelings are more likely to be prone to violence, either to themselves or others, because the words they use contain blame, which can lead to the creation of enemy images. Once an enemy image is created, it becomes easier to attack the one being blamed as we try to meet our needs for justice, respect, and consideration at the expense of their needs for autonomy, mutual consideration, safety, justice, and respect. This would be missing the mark of the heart, and it would be sin.

Using evaluative words isn't sin in and of itself; it's a reflection of our internal thinking that can lead to violence; what we do as a result makes the difference. NVC invites us to be gentle with our reactions when we hear evaluative words, responding empathetically while leaving out any moral judgment. It's best to accept the thoughts as they come and ask empathetic questions that lead back to the heart.

For example, I might say, "My best friend betrayed me by telling my secrets." *Betrayed* is evaluative, so I might substitute, "I'm telling myself that my friend betrayed me, and I'm feeling sad because my needs for trust and consideration aren't being met."

Here are some possible translations of evaluative words.

Evaluative Word	Possible Feelings	Possible Needs
Rejected	Disappointed, Sad, Hurt	Connection, Acceptance
Manipulated	Angry, Annoyed	Honesty, Respect
Abused	Sad, Hurt	Safety, Respect, Mutuality
Abandoned	Hurt, Sad, Depressed	Support, Belonging
Pressured	Scared, Annoyed, Anxious	Autonomy, Mutuality, Freedom
Misunderstood	Confused, Sad, Anxious	Understanding, Clarity
Neglected	Sad, Hurt, Angry	Caring, Support, Belonging

Figure 13. Translating Evaluative Words

Evaluative words may be common in everyday language, but they can destroy relationships. When we use such words, we aren't taking responsibility for our own experience; we're blaming others for it. Playing the victim implies a demand. It may not be verbalized, as we will see in the next chapter, but it's there nevertheless. The following exercise can help us to translate evaluative words we may be using.

Exercise

- What evaluative words on the list have you used? Choose one and write it here.

- How did you use the word? Use the space below to describe the circumstances.

- What feelings and needs might be behind the evaluative word in your story?

  Feeling _____ Need _____
  Feeling _____ Need _____
  Feeling _____ Need _____
  Feeling _____ Need _____

- Out of these feelings and needs, which combination most closely describes your experience and why?

Discussion

- With the group paired off, discuss with your partner your experience of the exercise.

- How difficult is it to identify evaluative words? Explain.

- Why do you think evaluative words are so prevalent?

- In light of Section II, Echoes of the Garden, discuss how evaluative words are related to the Fall, particularly Adam's response to God when God asked if they had eaten from the Tree of Judgment.

38.

Integrity: Examination of Conscience

The process of an examination of conscience combines Ignatian prayer[65] with 1 Corinthians 11:28-31. This general form of prayer has been traditionally used by Catholics and is being used increasingly by Protestants and Evangelicals.[66] I extend this form of prayer by incorporating the elements of NVC we've discussed so far.

I first learned of the examination of conscience from my seventh grade teacher, Hermano Eugenio La Paz at Colegio De La Salle in Bayamon, Puerto Rico. He said it was a way to discern God's will for us and that we must follow it, even if it goes against other people's beliefs and possibly even against the law. I was struck by his strong words, for they met my needs for authenticity and autonomy. Today, I continue to believe that this process, in general, enables me to find the requisite clarity of thought to make decisions that are in harmony with God, with others, and with my own heart.

There is also a healing element to this process; time seems to become less and less relevant the closer I am to God. I can spend a tremendous amount of time in mourning because of the effect of the judgments I have on myself and others. However, I find that as I let go of judgment, the desolate periods of time for healing seem to get shorter. As I get closer to God, I am also able to heal wounds from the past, as if the healing were taking place back when the pain occurred; I experienced this kind of restoration with my dad.

Traditionally, conscience refers to our ability to determine right from wrong. With NVC, the stories of creation and the Fall in Genesis invite us to let go of *right* and *wrong* thinking in favor of looking at strategies as more effective and less effective in meeting our needs—to make value judgments instead of moral judgments. Note that the generally accepted definitions of conscience below use a moral judgment paradigm, which is a direct result of the Fall.

This chapter defines *sin* as *missing the mark* and uses our hearts as guides instead of external rules. Here are two definitions of conscience from online dictionaries.

Dictionary.com

1. The inner sense of what is right or wrong in one's conduct or motives, impelling one toward right action; to follow the dictates of conscience.

2. The complex of ethical and moral principles that controls or inhibits the actions or thoughts of an individual.

Thefreedictionary.com

1a. The awareness of a moral or ethical aspect to one's conduct, together with the urge to prefer right over wrong: *Let your conscience be your guide.*

1b. A source of moral or ethical judgment or pronouncement; a document that serves as the nation's conscience.

1c. Conformity to one's own sense of right conduct; a person of unflagging conscience.

2. The part of the superego in psychoanalysis that judges the ethical nature of one's actions and thoughts and then transmits such determinations to the ego for consideration.

Thomas Bohenkotter writes

> The term *conscience* is not found in the Bible until the late Book of Wisdom, but the reality it refers to is found in many passages. The most favored term for it is *heart*, as in the expression *God probes the heart*.[67]

The usage of the word *heart* in this book is closer to the original meaning of the word, for the heart is where God left his image in us, and our needs vocabulary points back to this original gift.

One purpose of the conscience is to determine what actions to take and what actions to avoid. When it comes to decision making, traditionally, our choices are based on a standard of behavior which can take the form of a list of rules and is often described as *legalism*. Instead, this chapter defines a process of introspection using the heart as a guide.

An examination of conscience can be used to review events in the past and to help with decision making in the future. Usually done in solitude, examining our conscience may also be facilitated by a close friend, a counselor, or a spiritual director. The key is that trust, safety, and expression needs are met. Below, I've outlined the steps to examining our conscience using the concepts presented in this book. Below each step, I include a personal example to illustrate the process.

1. Find a Safe Space

Find a quiet place, free of distractions, in which it is safe to be yourself. You might light a candle, close the door, turn off the phones, and alert your household to your desire to remain undisturbed for a period of time — say thirty minutes.

- My safe place is typically in my living room, in front of the fireplace, sitting on the floor, looking North outside my window toward the San Bernardino mountains.

2. Let Go: Be Still and Know That I Am God

Psalms 46:10 invites us to let go of our worries and concerns of daily life, to quiet our minds, and to be open to the Holy Spirit. Pray for God's guidance.

- I love the spirit of this Psalm, as it helps me to settle down. I often focus on slow, deep breathing to assist in letting go of my busy schedule and becoming present in the moment.

3. Observe and Identify

Observe and identify your specific actions, choices, or areas of concern related to people, places, or things, without judgment. Be specific and keep your list short. Describe what happened the moment you experienced a strong jolt from your heart. On a piece of paper, list the issues you'd like to explore. Stick to the facts without evaluations or judgments. Do not list feelings or needs.

- During my divorce, the opposing attorney made the following offer: your son Alex and his mother Yaremi move from California to Texas. Alex flies back to California to spend a week with you every month; the cost comes out of spousal support.
- The California court system has a bias toward awarding the mother physical custody 90% of the time.

- I decided to settle out of court, and accepted their offer; I stayed in California.

4. Identify Judgments

Identify judgments you have made of yourself and others—anytime you were telling yourself that someone did something right or wrong. Inner criticism is especially important to identify. Accept whatever thoughts you've had in the past as part of the life journey. Be gentle and caring with yourself, and try not to judge yourself for judging.

- I am telling myself "I should have fought in court to keep him in California."
- I am also telling myself "I should move back to Texas."

5. Introspection: Our Educator

Our educator is the part of us that wants to learn something from our choices, the part that has concerns or regrets around strategies we've chosen or even options we're considering for the future. This might have taken the form of a judgment identified above; instead, identify the feelings and needs behind your judgments.

- I'm angry because my needs for fairness and justice are not being met.
- I'm angry because I'd like my needs as a father to be valued as much as Alex's mother's needs.
- I'm concerned that my son's needs are not being supported by the legal system, or being considered by his mother—I'd like to support and contribute to my son's well-being.
- I'm feeling concerned that as his dad, I have the unique opportunity to make a meaningful contribution in his life, and that I need more time together to fully support his development.

- I'm feeling sad that I don't get to see my son as often as I'd like — I miss connecting and playing with him.

6. Introspection: Our Chooser

The chooser is the part of us that motivates actions and choices based on concern for our own needs. If considering something in the past, figure out the motivation behind the choices made in the form of feelings and needs. If considering a choice to be made, determine the feelings and needs that would support each choice.

- I chose to settle out of court, to accept their offer to have them move away to Texas

  o Out of a concern for Alex's needs if his mother was unhappy and resentful all the time — my desire to contribute to a healthy environment for them.

  o Deep inside, I had a need for mutuality, in which all of our needs could be met, given what I knew about all of us, and the options before me.

  o Out of a sense of protecting my limited financial resources, and my ability to support myself.

- I liked my job as a communication systems engineer doing research and development on cutting edge wireless systems; my needs for contribution, growth and adventure were being met.

- I chose to stay in California because my heart comes alive there, and it would otherwise die — and I wouldn't be much of a Dad without my heart. The weather is great, and there is a lot of natural beauty to explore. I liked my friends there; I enjoyed a sense of community and belonging. My needs for autonomy and freedom were met by choosing to stay.

7. Consider the Needs of Others

Make a list of needs that are present or were present for others in your interactions. Remember, needs do not conflict. Problems arise only from differing strategies. You could list the strategies, but focus on the feelings and needs of the other people involved. Note that these are guesses that could be confirmed through conversation with the other.

- Yaremi's needs for comfortable and spacious shelter are better met in Texas because of the cost of living differences—more efficient use of financial support resources.

- Her needs for support and community would be more easily met because of existing friendships (we used to live there).

- Her needs for safety would more readily be met by a small Texas town vs. living in the Los Angeles area.

- Alex's needs for frequent quality time, emotional support and connection with his dad would not be met by a move away from his dad.

8. Mourn Needs Not Met

Mourn any needs not met by the strategies selected in the past, or to be chosen in the future. Also consider needs you are telling yourself will not be met and focus on the ones you value the most. Allow yourself to fully feel anything that comes up. Don't censor yourself, but honor your needs for integrity, authenticity, freedom, and expression.

- As I think about the choices I made back then, I feel some regret and sadness—wishing I had the tools, competence and understanding that I have now. I wish that I had known NVC back then.

- I'm feeling sad as I think of the impact the divorce had on Alex, around support, harmony, stability and cooperation needs not being met as well as I'd like.

- I feel some regret at not fully acknowledging and hearing Yaremi's needs, while also acknowledging my own—a sense of mutuality, where we both mattered and were able to communicate from the heart.

9. Celebrate the Gift of Needs, Express Gratitude

Celebrate any needs met, and also celebrate the needs not met by the various choices. All needs, met or unmet, are part of who we are as created beings. Needs are an expression of the gift of life within us; they remind us of God's love for us. They are beautiful even when not met. Consider your needs one at a time and ask God to reveal what you are meant to learn or to hear from the situation you are reviewing. Ask, "God, please give me clarity and wisdom regarding what is before me." After speaking, listen; sit with the beauty of the needs identified. Don't rush this step; take time to fully celebrate, and express any gratitude that comes up.

- Most of this step is done quietly, without writing, but I share some of what has come up for me to facilitate understanding the process.

- I pray and listen as I celebrate the needs identified. I imagine what God intended to communicate by creating my heart with these various facets:

  o Fairness, justice, support, contribution, meaning, connection, play, stability, acceptance, mutuality, protection, adventure, comfort, aliveness, beauty, community, belonging, autonomy, freedom.

- By being more whole and healthy, I model integrity and stability for Alex by living in harmony with my values.

- I celebrate my close relationship with Alex, as we continue to connect, grow and do fun things together in both California and Texas. I listen to his heart, and support him in spite of our geographical distance.

- Alex looks forward to traveling to his home in California during his time off school, and so do I. We share in the adventures, and beauty of the West Coast. I travel frequently to Texas during the school year.

- I am grateful for the feedback I've received from coaches, other parents, and his first boss concerning how Alex is respectful, considerate of others, and contributes to a positive team spirit.

- I am grateful for the relationship that I now have with his mother. We are better able to co-parent than we did before. I am grateful that sometimes his Texas family includes me in their activities, invites me to stay with them and helps me to feel welcome.

- I'm grateful for the conscious competence I've achieved in communicating, especially considering where I started. I celebrate my new ability to offer potentially meaningful contributions to Alex.

- My new growth and awareness helps me to consider other people's needs as important as my own—that I live in an abundant world of endless possibility—that I can rely on God as my source of life and provide for my needs—directly and through other people.

10. Pray for Reconciliation

Pray for guidance toward reconciliation with others, for forgiveness of sins, and for a restoration of peace. Pray specifically that God's will be done.

- Dear God—I thank you for the wonderful life experiences that come before me, and the learning that takes place as a result.

Thank you for encouraging me to reconnect to my heart and other people, and to be able to experience a taste of agape love as a dad to Alex. Please help me to listen carefully to his mother, and to empathize with her heart, and to speak my truth with clarity and grace through empathy and honesty. Give me the strength and compassion to engage her in a life-long conversation of forgiveness and peace, as we make choices on behalf of the interests and needs of our son. Help me to be a loving parent and to listen for your spirit as I co-parent Alex from a distance.

I celebrate all the wonderful things you have placed in my heart, and the clarity I now have to make choices consistent with your heart and love for me. Please give me clarity and wisdom to continue the path before me as a parent, and a member of your body—help me to discern your will in everything I do. Help me to fully embrace your love, and to contribute to the well-being of others. I lift these things up to you in the spirit of Christ Jesus, Amen.

11. Listen to the Holy Spirit; Find New Strategies

Having gone through the previous steps, acknowledging the needs of all parties involved, open yourself to the guidance of the Holy Spirit. Listen for strategies to meet everyone's needs. If a solution isn't forthcoming, consider making a list of options for further examination. Be open to possibilities.

12. Talk to Someone

After completing the previous steps, consider talking to close and trusted friends regarding what came up for you in the process. If others are involved in your issue, consider inviting them into a conversation of empathy and honesty. If talking has proved difficult in the past, consider the aid of a counselor, pastor, or NVC mediator. Focus on letting go of any strategies and "right" and "wrong" thinking. Given that this examination has helped you to connect with your own heart, start by listening empathetically to the needs alive in the other person — be present to them, acknowledge their feelings and needs, sometimes using words.

After sufficiently hearing the other person, ask if they are willing to hear your heart. Give your honesty, expressing your feelings and the needs behind them; use gentle requests to see if they were able to hear what you intended. The goal of the conversation is mutual understanding. If we are willing to be open to hearing each other's hearts, the Holy Spirit will do the rest.

The process defined in this chapter is based on ideas that have been around for centuries; the next chapter defines NVC processes of self-empathy that can be very useful in the examination of conscience and in everyday living.

39.

Inner Peace: Self-Empathy

This chapter puts OFNR into practice through self-empathy, which is the foundation of connection. The processes presented can be used to compliment an examination of conscience or be used alone. It is a practical way for us to fully accept God's grace and truth for us in this moment. We must be connected to our hearts before we can connect with others. OFNR helps us identify the things we tell ourselves, freeing us from the grip of judgment. Getting clear with our heart's feelings and needs helps us to become more presently conscious and alive. After connecting to our own feelings and needs, we begin to feel peaceful, light, and compassionate—the Holy Spirit is alive and well within us.

In this chapter, we'll review four self-empathy processes. I've given them names on behalf of my need for ease, clarity in identifying them, while acknowledging the original contributor's last name.

The first process, called the *Mackenzie Wrap*, is especially helpful when we're having a lot of judgments about ourselves or others. It incorporates a feedback loop that helps us go deeper into an issue by uncovering layers of emotions.

The second process, the *Rosenberg Classic*, is helpful for those just being introduced to NVC.

The third process, the *Gonzales Squares*, is helpful for those who have only one or two events to process and for those who are helped by spatial associations.

The fourth process, the *Manske Flow*, is helpful for people who are familiar with the vocabulary of needs. It can quickly help us to identify our core needs in the heat of the moment.

The following illustrations provide a snapshot of each self-empathy process. The circles represent states of awareness in which we focus our attention in a certain way. The letter J represents our judgments, O is observations, F is feelings, N is needs, and R is requests.

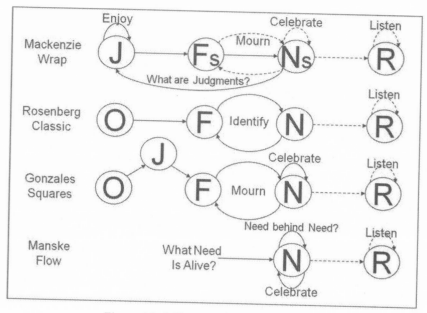

Figure 14. Self-Empathy State Diagrams

1. Mackenzie Wrap

I learned of this process at a weekend retreat called *Empathy as a Way of Being*,[68] facilitated by Mary Mackenzie in Laguna Beach. I like this process because it helps me to deal with judgments and allows me to go deeper into my heart. This is Mary's description of wrapping, with a few modifications of mine. She uses *jackal* as a metaphor for our judgments of ourselves and others. The letters in parentheses refer to the circles in the Self-Empathy State Diagrams.

1. *Enjoying the Jackal Show (J).* Give your jackals an opportunity to say all they want to say. If you try to

restrain the jackal, you might miss the full wisdom they hold for you. For example:

- He is so insensitive!
- What an insensitive slob!
- He never thinks about me!

2. *Feelings (F)*. Be aware of your feelings associated with the stimulus.

   - I feel angry and hurt and exasperated and annoyed.
   - And I'm embarrassed because I don't like sitting in restaurants alone.

3. *Making a Conscious Effort:* Make a conscious effort to translate jackal thoughts into self-empathy by moving on to the next steps.

4. *Needs (N)*. Be sure to identify your needs. If you get stuck in observations and feelings, you won't receive the relief and healing you desire. The full healing comes from identifying and mourning your unmet needs.

   - I need respect and predictability and accountability.

5. *More Jackals (J)*. The jackal has more to say. After recognizing the needs, I ask myself, *What judgments am I having now?* I repeat the process by going back to step 1, Enjoying the Jackal Show.

   - I've been waiting here for an hour!
   - Doesn't he value my time?

6. After wrapping back to the jackals a few times, I become clear on the feelings and needs that are close to my experience. If I start to repeat the same feelings and needs, it's a good time to go to step 7 and slow down the process. If I notice that I'm feeling strong emotions, I go into Mourning in Giraffe.

7. *Mourning in Giraffe (F)(N)*. Recognize the depth and sadness of the unmet need.

- When I think about all the waiting I've done in my life, I feel sad.

- I waited for John, waited for my mother, waited for my sister, and waited for my first husband.

- Sometimes they didn't show up at all.

- I really wanted predictability and respect. Yeah, that's it. I so long for respect and predictability.

- I need confidence and trust that when I make appointments with people, they'll show up.

- I just feel so sad when I think about how important this is to me and how rarely this need has been met.

Once you identify the feelings behind the unmet needs, sit with the feelings and mourn the times the needs weren't met. This is part of the healing process.

8. *Celebrate the Beauty Behind the Need (N)*. Notice if you feel a kind of shift when you have identified and fully mourned the unmet need. Put your attention on the need itself. Focus on its beauty and how wonderful it is to have that need met in your life.

- How would it feel, or how has it felt, to have your needs for predictability and trust fully met?

9. *Making a Request of Ourselves (R)*. Now that you have identified the true unmet need, what action would meet that need? Sometimes no action is called for, because identifying and mourning the unmet need is healing enough. At other times we might want to make a request.

- Would I be willing to spend the next fifteen minutes making a list of boundaries or limits that would satisfy my needs for predictability and trust?

- Would I be willing to verbalize my honesty tomorrow before dinner with John and explore strategies to meet both of our needs?

The following worksheet shows this process of self-empathy. The left-to-right J-F-N and wrapping process can be repeated as many times as necessary in order to get clear with your experience. Once you get clear, be sure to spend enough time mourning the needs not met. I have found the most healing by sharing this mourning with a close friend or someone else I trust. When I share the results of my self-empathy, I begin to experience the power of honesty as my personal truth is acknowledged by another person.

Judgments	Feelings	Needs
≻I keep having to talk with this damn computer	≻Despair ≻Annoyance	≻Freedom of expression ≻To be heard
≻I'm trapped ≻My job is holding me down	≻Anger ≻Sadness	≻To matter ≻Connection ≻To contribute ≻Purpose
≻I have to follow the rules ≻I need more training ≻I don't have any f* credentials	≻Lightness ≻Humor	≻Autonomy ≻Freedom ≻Competence ≻Life

Figure 15. Mackenzie Wrap Sample Worksheet

2. Rosenberg Classic Applied to Self-Judgment

This process is based on self-empathy as set forth in *Nonviolent Communication: A Language of Life*[69] and is extended to show how empathy can be used to deal with negative self-judgments. Self-judgment is important enough to be treated separately because of its damaging effects on our life experience.

There are times when we may not be aware of our negative self-judgments. They may be hidden, because we're so used to them that they function as blind spots. Metaphorically, it's as if the serpent from the Garden were doing its best to hide the truth from us so that we continue to eat from the Tree of Judgment.

People practicing NVC call these negative self-judgment thoughts *jackals*. The jackal represents the part of us that judges and labels people, keeping us isolated, disconnected, and unable to enjoy a life of abundance. These jackal thoughts can be directed toward others or toward ourselves. Becoming aware of our jackals is extremely important in NVC.

We often have jackal thoughts about ourselves. These can be highly destructive, because they often are hidden. They keep us from fully living and loving, and when projected outward they can be the source of violence directed at others. When projected inward, they can be the source of violence to ourselves. Here is a list of common jackal thoughts.

- I'm not good
- I'm not lovable
- I don't have enough
- I can't do it
- I'm too heavy
- I'm too thin

- I'm ugly
- I'm stupid
- I'm too short
- I'm too tall
- Nobody likes me
- I'm [any label]

Rather than just replace these thoughts with other thoughts, which is what positive affirmations do, we can strive to transform them by inviting them to integrate into the beauty of our needs,[70] resting in God's love for us. This is the goal of the following exercise.

Exercise

1. A good way to identify jackals is to write down the story around an issue you have. After finishing the story, using a different colored pen, underline all the judgments. Then, on a separate piece of paper, make a list of all your jackal thoughts. Work with one at a time, using this or any other self-empathy process in this chapter.

2. Empathize with the jackal thought by guessing at some of the feelings and needs behind it, repeating the process at least three times. I find it useful to match each feeling with a need, but sometimes multiple feeling words and multiple needs match the experience. Do whatever works for you. The reference sheet of feelings and needs at the end of this book may be helpful in completing this step.

Feeling(s) _____ Need(s) _____

Feeling(s) _____ Need(s) _____

Feeling(s) _____ Need(s) _____

Feeling(s) _____ Need(s) _____

Feeling(s) _____ Need(s) _____

Feeling(s) _____ Need(s) _____

3. As you guess at feelings and needs, stay aware of your mood and watch for any changes.

- You might experience an emotional release—a moment of catharsis. Let yourself feel whatever emotions come up. Give yourself space and time to fully experience your feelings.

- After mourning for a sufficient amount of time, you may notice a shift to a more positive mood or a sense of physical relaxation.

- This feeling-need combination likely points to the unmet need of the jackal thinking. Circle this need for use in the remainder of the process.

  In the Rosenberg Classic process, we make a request of ourselves to meet the unmet need, and are done. When formulating strategies with our requests, we'd like to choose solutions that are in harmony with all our needs — this promotes a sense of well-being.

4. The process in steps 1–4 can be repeated as often as needed, as in the Mackenzie Wrap process.

This can continue until unmet needs are identified, or it can be the end of the exercise. I prefer to celebrate the beauty of needs. I have adapted the remainder of this process in the subsequent steps.

5. Hold the unmet need in your mind and begin to celebrate its beauty.

   - Think of a time when the need was met to your satisfaction, or

   - Imagine what it would look and feel like to have the need met to your complete satisfaction.

   - Write out the experience of having the need fully met. Be creative — have fun with it!

6. After getting sufficiently clear with a vision of our needs being fully met, invite the jackal thought into the same heart space as the celebration of the need. Contemplative imagery can be helpful; you might search for imagery that works for you, such as Anthony de Mello's books and contemplation exercises.[71] This exercise might help you create your own imagery.

- Find a safe space—a room, a park, a mountain, a deserted beach—where you can sit quietly and undisturbed for fifteen to thirty minutes.
- Sit in a comfortable position.
- Read the following lines or have someone read them aloud. Search for the deeper meaning behind the words. What do they point to? Pause for a minute or so after each line. Try to connect with the essence that the words convey.

You are loved by God, as you were created by him in his image.

God is love, and you have something of God within you.

You are God's loved one; you are special and unique in God's eyes.

Jesus came to bring you comfort and rest because of his love for you.

- Recall your vision around having your needs fully met.
- Contemplate the possibilities of God's intention in giving you these needs.
- Recall the jackal thought you wrote down earlier. Invite the jackal to hear the truth of God's message for you.
- If you find yourself distracted by your thoughts, focus on breathing deeply and slowly from your belly.
- Be gentle with yourself, starting with one-minute intervals at first. As the quiet listening of your breath feels more comfortable, begin to increase the amount of time to five, ten, fifteen, and even thirty minutes. This process can be part of a discipline of daily prayer and meditation.

- As you fully inhale, your torso expands; as you fully exhale, it contracts.

- Stay in this quiet space as long as you are able, or until you feel like your process is complete.

7. At the end of your contemplation time, write down your experience of this process. Consider adapting it to your own tastes.

8. Because we are so used to jackal thoughts, there are times when the jackals come back. Be gentle with yourself and return to any self-empathy process, noting any differences that may arise in your feelings and thoughts.

Our role is to be open to healing, to release the jackal thought into the care of God, to invite it into something better. We are a participant in this process, but we let go of the outcome even as we hang on to our heart needs. As we let go of our judgmental thinking, we may feel a sadness of letting go of something familiar; we take responsibility for our thoughts and judgments to invite the Holy Spirit to do the healing. Our job is to become aware, shine a light on the jackal, and let go of the outcome.

3. Gonzales Squares

I have attended some of Robert Gonzales's sessions on empathy[72] and have felt a lot of joy in connecting and learning. The following is a template for the steps in his empathy process; the six squares can be easily created by folding a sheet of paper in half the long way and then in thirds the short way. Write these steps in the squares to create your template. Then complete the steps in the order shown for your particular experience.

1. Observation (what you're reacting to, in one sentence)

4. Mourn the unmet needs (sink into the feelings and linger as long as you need to)

2. Your thoughts about the situation (judgment, blame, criticism)

5. Sit with the beauty of the needs (this happens automatically when you complete the mourning process)

3. Translate your thoughts into feelings and needs

6. Request (see if a request of yourself or the other person naturally arises)

4. Manske Flow

This last form of self-empathy from Jim and Jori Manske,[73] comes in handy as we try to stay self-connected during a situation in real time — in the moment that things are happening. The challenge of this process is that it requires knowing the language of needs — the words on the needs list. It takes time and practice to become fluent in the language of needs; this process is recommended after some time practicing NVC.

The process begins with the question, "What feeling and need are most alive?" Once we're clear in our mind what need is present, we ask the next question: "If that need were met, what other needs would be met?"

We continue asking that question until we notice a shift in mood, settle on a single need, or bounce between two similar needs. Mary Mackenzie suggests that the process naturally stops once we reach a core need (the boldfaced needs of Figure 11). Here's what the process looked like for me at a retreat.

Feeling: *Loneliness*

Needs Identified (my process)	Needs Summary (Reference)
• Connection	• Safety, Protection, Life, Trust
• Understanding	• To be valued as unique, to be Celebrated
• To be known	• Freedom, Autonomy, Choice
• Celebration	• To matter, to have a place at the table, Mutuality
• Touch	• To Contribute, Help, Support
• Play	• Play, Discovery, Learning
• Companionship	• Clarity, Understanding
• Rest	• Belonging, Community
• Aliveness	• Meaning, Purpose
• Contribution	• Self-acceptance, I'm okay, I'm good enough
• Meaning	• Faith, Hope, Trust in God
	• Love, Beauty, Celebration, Mourning

I started the process with the feeling that was alive in the moment: loneliness. I made that the title of my exercise. I began to identify my needs using the questions defined above, resulting with needs on the left column. On the column on the right, I list a summary of needs for reference—words that are related are grouped together.

Toward the end of my process, I cycled between *Contribution* and *Meaning*. The needs at the end of my process are also in my core needs list. The end of my process involved prayer and meditation, while focusing on the needs for contribution and meaning, listening to the guidance of the Holy Spirit. For me, the answer has been to continue with this book to see where it leads.

As we work these processes, we become aware that self-empathy is a discipline wherein we choose to facilitate our own understanding, working with the Holy Spirit and accept whatever healing takes place. These are processes that assist with taking care of our plank, as Jesus taught in Matthew 7.

We might struggle to get the clarity we need by ourselves because the situation stimulates some old pain, or we might be unable to facilitate our own process. During these times, it can be helpful to call a friend and ask if they would be willing to listen to us and give us empathy. Sometimes seeing a licensed therapist or counselor is the best course of action. We must do whatever we need to get help and support to acknowledge and process our feelings and needs, because freedom and life are on the other side.

If we receive help from someone else, we will know we have received enough empathy when we notice a shift in our mood. We might feel more relaxed, compassionate, and maybe curious about others and verbalize how we're feeling in the moment, giving our honesty.

At this point in the conversation, we might ask what's going on for the other person, perhaps asking "What comes up for you after hearing me say these things?" Instead of receiving empathy, we're now ready to offer it.

40.

Grace: Empathetic Listening

The concept of empathy as a form of grace was introduced in Section III, Sermon of the Master. It is essential to give ourselves empathy before offering it. We must fully accept God's grace and truth before we can extend it to others. If we have received enough empathy, then we can be present for someone else.

The intention of this section is to put the concepts of empathy and grace into practice. Empathy requires presence, accepting and respecting the unique experience of the person telling their story, and a caring and honoring of their life journey, which only they may know fully.

When offering empathy, we give our full attention to the other person. Sometimes silent empathy, when we just sit and listen, is the most helpful. When offering empathy to someone, we let go of preconceptions about the situation, and we approach every situation as new, with a beginner's childlike mind. Our voice quality and tone should be consistent with our intention to listen and understand.

Our role in offering empathy is to be a loving witness and to help the other person go deeper into their heart experience. We support them in what can be a scary, painful journey on a narrow path. On this journey into the heart, there are many obstacles that cause the person receiving empathy to fall off the path toward the heart. Usually it's a form of judgment, but it can also be due to a shift of focus away from the person telling the story.

Judgment and discomfort can look like nervous laughter — a joke, a change of subject to something totally new. Mary Mackenzie calls this *jackal block*. In this case, the person giving empathy just follows along by making observations and guessing at the feelings and needs of the speaker. You might say, "You just told a joke. Are you uncomfortable with the path we were on? Do you want some relief?"

I try to remain conscious and aware of whose needs are being considered in the moment. I make sure to let the other person guide the direction of the conversation, and I listen closely for the feelings and needs being expressed. The direction of flow in a conversation can change at any moment; awareness and initiative by the person offering empathy can hold the space and encourage further movement into the heart on both sides of the conversation.

When offering empathy, we may make observations about what is said by repeating it back directly or indirectly, such as, "When you said that your mother fed you and hugged you three times a day ..." or "When your father said, 'I want to provide for you and be supportive' ..." We might make observations of physical changes such as body posture, tone of voice, tears, or movements, such as, "I noticed that your eyes teared up a little when you said ..."

The observation may be omitted, and empathy can proceed directly to feelings and needs in the form of a request for information. When offering empathy, we ask the person receiving empathy to look inside and see if what we said is accurate for them. Empathy given is only a guess by the person offering it and doesn't have to be right in order to be helpful. What is important is the intention, not necessarily the words or the accuracy of the guesses. An inquiry about their heart might be, "Are you feeling _____ because you need _____?"

The feeling guessed at can be any word from the feeling list, and the need can be any word from the needs list. Empathy might sound like this.

Are you feeling joyful because your need for contribution is being met?

Are you sad because you want more intimacy and connection in your life?

Are you feeling <u>discouraged</u> and <u>annoyed</u> because you need more autonomy?

The structure above is most useful as a tool for learning. After some time using the process, empathy begins to sound more natural and flows within the conversation. This comes with patience, time, practice and a supportive group of fellow travelers. The best way to learn how to offer empathy is through an NVC practice group. If there isn't one in your area, you might consider starting your own.

When I was first learning NVC, I was often confused about who says what and when. The following sequence chart is intended to show the normal flow of a conversation when offering empathy, but it isn't a formula to be followed at all times. It's offered as a learning tool to clarify the dynamics of empathy. In the empathetic dialogue sequence illustrated below, Person A expresses themselves and Person B is the empathetic listener.

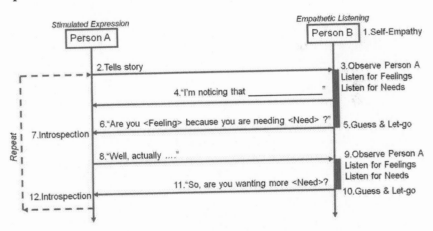

Figure 16. Empathy Sequence: A Receives Empathy from B

Twelve Steps of Empathy

1. B has enough self-empathy to be present with someone else
2. A tells their story
3. B observes A, listening for feelings and needs
4. B occasionally makes an observation (optional step)
5. B guesses at A's feelings and needs and lets go of the results of all the thinking, allowing A to naturally determine the direction of the conversation. This frees B to remain present to A while listening to what is being said (as opposed to having an agenda).
6. B occasionally verbalizes feelings and needs guesses to A in the form of questions
7. A looks inward to see if B's guesses work or not
8. A verbalizes whatever comes up as a result of introspection
9. B observes A, listening for feelings and needs
10. B makes a guess at A's feelings and needs and lets go of the recent thoughts
11. B verbalizes feelings and needs guesses to A in questions
12. A looks inward to see if B's guesses work or not.

The process above repeats itself for a while, until either A feels a shift in mood or B has a strong desire to express honesty. A's shift might be a sigh, a physical relaxation, or a catharsis (emotional release). After a shift occurs, A usually feels more tranquil, compassionate, and curious about B or the other person or people they are talking about.

B continues to offer empathy as long as they can be present; if not, then B expresses their honesty, gently stepping out of empathetic role by telling the other person they have run out of energy and cannot continue the conversation. If A has the resources to be empathetic, perhaps A can listen empathetically to B. In this fashion, the two support each other instead of the conversation being exclusively about either A or B.

The following exercise is designed for a group setting. Like learning how to dance, it helps to practice with different people.

Exercise (in a group)

- Think of a time recently when life was less than wonderful. Describe in the space below what happened the moment things changed from being okay to not okay. Don't worry about doing it right or using NVC, just write out what comes to mind in three to five minutes.

- Pair up with someone; if this is a repeat of the exercise, change partners. In each pair, pick who goes first using different criteria every time: A is the shorter, the younger, or perhaps the person who's wearing glasses. Have fun with it.

- A shares their story as B gives empathy by guessing at feelings and needs. Time this for five to eight minutes.

- Switch roles and do the exercise again for five to eight minutes.

Discussion

- Share with the larger group your feelings after completing the exercise. What needs were met? What needs were not met?

- Was the exercise difficult, easy, or somewhere in between? What made it so?

41.

Truth: Honest Expression

Giving honesty is as important as giving empathy; they are the two sides of the conversation. Honesty has been very difficult for me to give, especially to people I care about. After recognizing my discomfort and practicing in groups and with friends, I now see the value and importance of expressing my honesty. Without it, I start to feel resentful inside because my needs for self-respect and expression are not met.

I have been surprised at how well things turn out after expressing my honesty; this is when the elements of NVC come in most handy to me. I focus on delivering my observations, feelings, and needs, followed by a request. It might sound something like this.

I'm noticing the time is now 5:41, and we had agreed to meet at 5:00. I'm feeling a little annoyed because I want to use my time efficiently. Would you be willing to tell me what you heard me say?

The last time we went out for dinner was last December. I'm feeling discouraged because my needs for support and celebration aren't being met. I'm wondering, what comes up for you when you hear me say this?

In each case, it's important that the other person doesn't hear judgment, criticism or blame, which will be apparent if the reply to the request includes a judgment. If this happens, one might choose to briefly switch roles and offer empathy to the other person, before repeating our honesty using different words to make it clearer, hoping the other person hears the needs you expressed.

Like the previous illustration, the following sequence chart illustrates the dynamics of giving honesty. It is a learning aid, not a template for all situations.

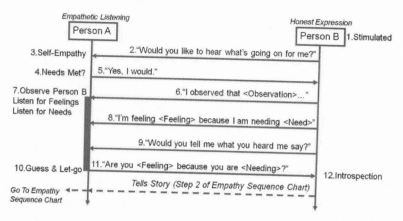

Figure 17. Honesty Sequence: Person A hears Honesty from B

Twelve Steps of Honest Expression

1. B is stimulated by A's actions or something else.

2. B requests to be heard (to express honesty).

3. A gives themselves empathy.

4. A checks in with themselves to see if their needs would be met by saying yes to B's request.

5. A replies with integrity, being true to themselves.

6. B shares an observation.

7. A observes B, listening for feelings and needs.

8. B expresses their feelings and needs.

9. B completes their honesty with a request.

10. A makes a guess at B's feelings and needs and then let's go of thoughts that came up.

11. A verbalizes a guess in the form of a question.

12. B looks inward to see if the guess was close.

After B's introspection, the dialogue sequence proceeds to the empathy sequence (Figure 16), starting with step 2, Tells Story. The following exercises provide practice for the empathy and honesty sequences.

Exercise: Classic OFNR Honesty

1. The first part of this exercise deals with clarifying our personal experience through self-empathy, and is to be completed by each person individually in five to eight minutes.

    - Think of a time when someone close to you did something that stimulated unpleasant feelings such as anger, sadness, or hurt when your needs were not met. If the event was lengthy or complex, pick the first recollection that comes to mind, or the simplest.

    - Describe what happened <u>at the moment</u> you felt the unpleasant feeling. Keep it brief and to the point.

    - Underline any judgments or evaluations in what you wrote.

    - Write an observation of what happened, without the judgments or evaluations.

    - What feelings were stimulated by the observation?

    - What needs were not met?

    - Which of the following connecting requests seems most appropriate? Select one, modify it, or come up with your own request.

      Would you be willing to tell me what you heard me say?

      Just to make sure you aren't hearing a judgment, would you tell me what you heard?

      I'm wondering what you heard me say.

2. Pair up with someone in the group. Decide who shares their honesty first and call them Person A.

- For three to five minutes, A will practice giving B their honesty by stating their observations, feelings, needs, and requests based on what they wrote earlier.

  B gives empathy by listening quietly, or briefly echoing the feelings and needs that were heard (keep it short, focus on A).

  Continue the conversation until A's needs are understood. Notice a body shift, a sigh, a lighter mood, or a statement that they're ready to continue. Give this three minutes.

  A might ask , "What comes up for you when you hear me say this?" See if anything was stimulated by what B heard.

- After three to five minutes, switch roles and repeat.

Exercise: Honest Expression through the Beauty of Needs

1. This exercise is an extension of the previous one; the first part is to be completed by each person individually.

   - Write down the needs you identified in the previous exercise below.

   - Pick one and imagine what it would be like to have this need *fully met*, drawing on past experience if you wish. There are no limits, think of what God might be able to do for you around meeting this need—be creative. Let go of all judgment. Take five to eight minutes to write down what you've imagined.

2. Pair up again, with A reading what was written above, focusing on celebrating the beauty of the need

   - A expresses honesty for three to five minutes

- B listens and gives brief empathy (echoing feelings and needs only) — keep focus on A.
- Switch roles after A is sufficiently heard or after the allotted time.

Discussion

- Discuss with the larger group how you are feeling at the moment. What needs are met? What needs are unmet?
- Did you perceive a difference between the two forms of honesty in the exercises? What was different?
- What was the most difficult part of the exercise? What was the easiest part?
- Did giving honesty this way seem artificial or did it flow naturally?

42.

Balancing Empathy and Honesty

The purpose of this chapter is to highlight the need for balance in our dialogues, given that we all want mutually satisfying connections. People are usually more comfortable in one of the two roles. I've noticed that I'm more comfortable listening empathetically than expressing my honesty.

Seeing a need for balance and full connection motivates us to switch roles every now and then in any conversation. This is demonstrated by the dialogue sequence diagram in Figure 18, in which Person B starts giving their honesty while Person A offers empathy. The dashed line in the diagram demonstrates that at any point in the conversation, either side may request a role transition; after a mutual agreement is achieved, A begins to express honestly their experience while B begins offering empathy. This diagram demonstrates a flow in conversation that begins to feel natural once we have a little practice in an NVC group.

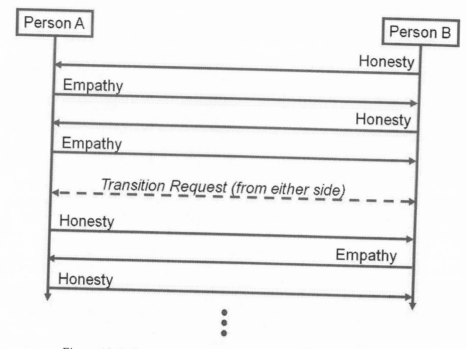

Figure 18. Balancing Empathy and Honesty Dialogue Sequence

The dialogue above can be easily contrasted with the conversations that are typical when empathy is not present. The diagram below presents such a sequence, where each person speaks almost in desperation to be heard, while the other person is just waiting for the right time to interrupt to speak. Each person takes turns interrupting, and in many instances changing the subject to match their own experience.

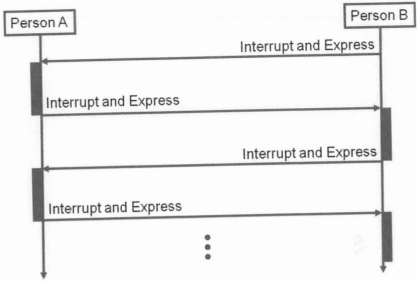

Figure 19. Desperate Expression Sequence Diagram

There's nothing wrong with this kind of conversation, it's just important to note the differences. Sometimes this can be fun too—each person matching something that was said to their own personal experience. I have observed this pattern to be common in groups of people. After about fifteen minutes, I tend to tire of the pop-corn style group sharing and begin noticing discomfort and disappointment as I want more depth of connection.

Discussion

- Comment on your experience of the two kinds of dialogues presented in this section. How often do you experience each, and how do you feel afterward?

- Do you ever get bored, desperate to be heard, or frustrated with pop-corn style group sharing? Describe what comes up for you in those instances.

- What kind of conversations would you like to have, and what is keeping you from having them?

- When considering empathy and honesty, which role is more comfortable for you?
  - Guess at the needs you are meeting by your dominant role.
  - What needs are not being met by staying within your comfort zone?
  - What request do you have for yourself after considering the information in this chapter?

43.

Openness: Listen for the Strategy, Follow the Spirit

After a connection is complete between two people, when each person has received empathy and given their honesty and both sides are feeling joyful, grateful, or hopeful — sit and celebrate for a while in your shared experience — then it's time to be open to strategies. It's important always to remember the needs that have been expressed and are alive in the conversation. Sometimes the needs shift as a result of our connection. Hold onto whatever needs are present in the moment, and be willing to explore different strategies to meet them.

Achieving a symphony of mutual understanding is the goal of Compassionate Connecting. At this point in the conversation, when we are experiencing the joy of being fully connected, we stand back and listen. Jesus said he would show up at times like these, when people gather in his name and have a heart connection.

> *"Again, I tell you that if two of you on earth agree about anything you ask for, it will be done for you by my Father in heaven. For where two or three come together in my name, there am I with them." (Matthew 18:19–20)*

This is when the reward for all the hard work of the conversation comes to fruition. Metaphorically, this is when we get to share in the mystical Body of Christ and to eat from the Tree of Life. Listen for the whisper of God's voice, the voice who wants everyone to experience love and compassion. The source of all that is, the great *I AM* made an abundant universe filled with endless possibilities.

Exercise

- Next time you're in a dialogue with someone and you've worked hard to identify the needs alive in each other, sit together quietly and hold the needs gently in your awareness. It sometimes helps to write them down on a piece of paper and place the paper somewhere you can see it.

- Listen for the voice of the Holy Spirit. Ask for help. Celebrate the beauty of what God has given you in your heart, which is represented by your needs, and let the Spirit do the rest.

V.

CONVERSATIONS IN CLOSING

Sometimes I wonder if God wants us to struggle before we get to appreciate the gifts of our life journey—is this part of our experience of the breadth and depth of God's love for us—of the vast greatness of his creation? Is there something for me to learn from this moment?

My sense is that God wants us to experience the abundance of the Kingdom available to us right now. All he asks is that we love him, and love others as ourselves—which may look like: slow down, accept reality as it is, remove our own plank, help our friends with their specks, and give love a chance to take hold. A life filled with a clear awareness and celebration of our experience and an appreciation, respect, and compassion for others is a life lived in harmony with the spirit of Christ.

The Kingdom, the pearl, and the treasure in the middle of the field are available to those who are willing to walk the path of grace and truth of Jesus Christ. NVC helps us put those principles into practice as a discipline of love in conversation. My hope is that you are motivated to try it out in real life.

I am grateful that you made it to the end of the book, supporting my needs for expression, my livelihood and to be known. My wish is that it helps bring more joy, peace and fulfillment to your life—hearing that it did would allow me to celebrate with you, meeting my needs for contribution, meaning and connection. Would you be willing to tell me?[74]

44.

Scripture Translations to Inspire

It all arose out of a Conversation, a Conversation within God.

In fact, the Conversation was God.

God started the discussion and everything came out of this, and nothing happened without consultation.

This was the life – the life that was the light of men shining in the darkness, a darkness which neither understood nor quenched its creativity.

John, a man sent by God, came to remind people about the nature of the light so that they would observe.

He was not the subject under discussion but the bearer of an invitation to join in.

The subject of the Conversation, the original light, came into the world, the world that had arisen out of his willingness to converse.

He fleshed out the words but the world did not understand. He came to those who knew the language, but they did not respond.

Those who did became a new creation (his children); they read the signs and responded.

These children were born out of sharing in the creative activity of God.

They heard the Conversation still going on, here, now, and took part, discovering a new way of being people.

To be invited to share in a Conversation about the nature of life, was for them, a glorious opportunity not to be missed.

(John 1:1-14 Clive Scott[75])

Once, having been asked by the Pharisees when the kingdom of God would come, Jesus replied, "The kingdom of God does not come with your careful observation, nor will people say, 'Here it is,' or 'There it is,' because the kingdom of God is within you." (Luke 17:20–21, NIV)

And I will ask the Father, and he will give you another Counselor to be with you forever – the Spirit of truth. The world cannot accept him, because it neither sees him nor knows him. But you know him, for he lives with you and will be in you. I will not leave you as orphans; I will come to you. Before long, the world will not see me anymore, but you will see me. Because I live, you also will live. On that day you will realize that I am in my Father, and you are in me, and I am in you. (John 14:16–20, NIV)

Nonviolent Communication (NVC) by Marshall Rosenberg invites us to re-frame how we express ourselves and hear others by focusing on what we are Observing, Feeling, Needing and Requesting (OFNR)

Observations vs. Evaluations

•An Observation is the act of seeing or noticing something with unbiased attention
•An Evaluation adds a subjective experience, judgment or criticism

Feelings vs. Thoughts

•Feelings tell us if our needs are being met or not. We experience pleasant feelings when needs are met, unpleasant feelings when needs not met (see back page)
•Thoughts are the products of mental activity: (i.e. evaluations, analysis, beliefs, comparisons, opinions, judgments) – masquerade: "I feel *like* ____ " is a thought

• **Common *Evaluative* Words which Sound like Feelings**
(Not Feelings as they imply that someone else has power over you – i.e. a "victim" strategy)
Rejected, Betrayed, Manipulated, Abused, Abandoned, Used, Victimized, Pressured, Misunderstood, Neglected, Coerced, Underpaid, Cornered, Intimidated, Bullied, Inadequate, Distrusted, Boxed-in, Unappreciated, Isolated, Overworked, Patronized, Pushed Away, Picked-on, Let-down, Attacked, Blamed, Criticized, Harassed, Left-out

Needs (Values, Desires) vs. Strategies (Wants)

• Needs are a part of us which seeks fulfillment (see back page)
• A Strategy describes a doable action to be taken with the hopes of meeting a need

• **Strategies are Often Confused with Needs**:
"I want to see this movie" (e.g. entertainment), "I need some chocolate" (e.g. comfort?), "I need to go to Yoga" (e.g. health, rest?), "I need a beer" (e.g. relaxation?), "I need you" (e.g. connection?), "I need to buy a sexier car" (e.g. to be seen, acceptance?), "I need to go dancing" (e.g. play, celebration?), ...

Requests vs. Demands
• A Demand is when a specific outcome must be achieved ("No" not ok)
• A Request is a clear description of what someone can do to meet a need of yours (i.e. must be doable)

1. Would you be willing to tell me what *you heard me* say?
2. How do you *feel* when you hear me say this?
3. Would you be willing to brainstorm on some strategies?

Empathy is being present* with someone, listening and reflecting *feelings* and *needs* (a form of *Grace*)

"Are you Feeling____ because you are Needing____?"

- *Presence through Self-Empathy
  - Silent Empathy, Just Listen
  - Intention is most important
  - Curiosity, Caring, Voice Quality
  - Full Attention
  - Goal is to give Understanding
- Not to be used as formula on others, mostly for learning
  - Words are optional
- Observation and Request are optional when sharing empathy
- Focus on the Beauty of Needs
  - Think of a time when need was fully met

NOT EMPATHY

- Giving Advise: "I think you should ___"
- One-upping: "That's nothing; wait till you hear..."
- Educating: "This could be good for you."
- Consoling: "It wasn't your fault; you did your best."
- Story-telling: "That reminds me when ..."
- Shutting Down: "Don't feel so bad!"
- Sympathizing: "I feel ___ when..."
- Interrogating: "When did this begin?"
- Explaining: "I would have called but ..."
- Correcting: "That's not how it happened."

Honesty is expressing to another person what is going on inside ourselves (OFNR), in a way which maintains our connection with them (a form of *Truth*)

- Being "Authentic" rather than just being "Nice"
- Best Connection: **Empathy before Honesty** (1.Oneself, 2.Others)
- Honesty is not a way to guarantee that we get what we want, but a way to clearly express what we are experiencing (i.e. alive in us).
  - Important to let go of the outcome (i.e. wanted strategy)

- **Observation**: "I'm observing that _____."
- **Feeling/Need**: "I'm feeling _____ because I'm needing _____."
- **Request**
  1. Would you be willing to tell me what you heard me say?
  2. How do you feel when you hear me say this?
  3. Would you be willing to explore some strategies to meet both our needs (i.e. brainstorm solutions)?

Feelings tell us if Needs are being met or not

Feelings When Needs Are Met

- Happy
- Joyful
- Grateful
- Touched
- Hopeful
- Excited
- Delighted
- Inspired
- Amazed
- Enchanted

- Relieved
- Peaceful
- Centered
- Relaxed
- Content
- Pleased
- Comfortable
- Satisfied
- Alive
- Passionate
- Compassion

Feelings When Needs Not Met

- Sad
- Afraid
- Anxious
- Upset
- Worried
- Embarrassed
- Hurt
- Depressed
- Cranky
- Annoyed
- Resentful
- Angry
- Confused

- Jealous
- Unhappy
- Disappointed
- Discouraged
- Bored
- Lonely
- Guilty
- Ashamed
- Torn
- Suspicious
- Vulnerable
- Frustrated
- Numb

Needs something required for Life – Life to the full

- Needs are universal – we all have them – they are not in conflict with each other
- We are born with needs – they are a gift from God which makes us human

- **Survival**
  - Sustenance
  - Shelter
  - Procreation
  - Nurturance
- **Protection**
  - Security
  - Safety
  - Justice
  - Respect
  - Consideration
- **Meaning**
  - Purpose
  - Contribution
  - Competence
  - Integrity

- **Autonomy**
  - Freedom
  - Choice
  - Creativity
  - Empowerment
- **Interdependence**
  - Cooperation
  - Community
  - Inclusion
  - Mutuality
  - Support
- **Honesty**
  - Authenticity
  - Self-Connection
  - Self-Expression
  - Clarity
  - Learning

- **Well-Being**
  - Healing
  - Peace
  - Balance
  - Ease
  - Trust
- **Empathy**
  - To be known
  - Understanding
  - Connection
  - Acceptance
  - Affection
  - Acknowledgement
  - Intimacy
  - Love

- **Regeneration**
  - Rest
  - Celebration
  - Mourning
  - Leisure
  - Play
- **Transcendence**
  - Presence
  - Beauty
  - Harmony
  - Flow
  - Space
  - Hope, Faith
  - Life

Needs are often confused with Strategies!

45.

Epilogue

As I was writing the manuscript for this book, I had to make several decisions regarding what to include and how to include certain information for my audience. This book was primarily intended for followers of Christ, anyone interested in Nonviolent Communication, and anyone searching for ways of integrating the teachings of Jesus into their interpersonal communications. At the same time, I didn't want to write a book that caused more division in the world. So, I asked a couple of people who were not Christian to review my book. They brought up two main issues: God expressed as male, and how to relate to people that do not follow Christ.

Christian tradition speaks of God in the male form based on the cultural preferences of the Jewish tradition — the root of Christianity. The God of my understanding transcends the human trait of gender. The author of Genesis states that "male and female he created them" in God's image (Genesis 1:27); thus God is neither male nor female, but something of both. I am torn about how to meet everyone's needs while still meeting the objectives of the book; I want to show consideration, a sense of mutuality, and I desire to contribute to healing gender discrimination. Because of the intended audience, the scriptures that I quoted are based on the popular NIV and NLT Bibles, which present God in the male form. I maintained the gender usage of these translations out of a desire for connection to the primary audience, clarity, and ease of expression.

One of my reviewers expressed some sadness after reading the first two sections of my manuscript because she wondered how my book related to people who were not Christian, who followed other paths — her needs for inclusion, growth, and connection were not met. She wondered if I could find a way to consider the rest of humanity. I resonated with her needs and realized that my own needs for contributing to peace would not be met if my book led to throwing rocks and building more walls instead of bridges. I didn't know how to meet these needs given my personal history, intended audience, and the inspiration I get from Jesus. I wanted to be able to speak authentically from my life experience without alienating the rest of the planet. I held on to those needs and became willing to listen for a way forward. This is what came out of my prayer.

I'm a communications engineer and a *Star Trek* fan. In case you're from another planet and haven't heard of it, it's a science-fiction TV series created by Gene Roddenberry that tells a story of humanity several centuries in the future from the perspective of the crew of the starship *Enterprise*. Their advanced civilization has conquered disease, poverty and achieved interstellar travel, teleportation, fusion, and world peace. Their technology is so advanced that they also developed a universal translator; this device listens to sounds, compares them to a library of known languages, and automatically— almost instantaneously—translates them into the native language of the user. I hypothesize (because I haven't seen an episode on this topic) that the universal translator was a key enabling technology that facilitated the end of war on Earth and the beginning of a new era in which all humans had the chance of living life to its fullest, with the only limitations being their talents, their will, and the choices they made.

I am convinced that Nonviolent Communication (NVC) is the root enabling technology that facilitates the co-creation of the universal translator in this world. The only difference is that instead of computers doing the translation, human beings willing to practice this discipline of love in conversation do it. Mastery of this discipline enables us to see things that were previously hidden, to be present in situations that were previously difficult, and to relate to people we previously considered enemies. My hope is that it would facilitate a mutual understanding of the heart among Muslims, Jews, and Christians—allowing us to find much to celebrate in our common ancestry from Abraham, to value and respect our unique traditions, and to open up the possibility for collaboration in finding ways to reform our societies in service of our common humanity, in service of God. NVC also facilitates connection between and within religious and nonreligious people.

My software development background suggests a description of this book as *The Universal Translator Interface to Christianity*. That can be translated for my audience as *The Way of Christ through Nonviolent Communication*. I envision many other interfaces being written.

Notes

1 Source: *Nonviolent Communication: A Language of Life* by Marshall Rosenberg, 2003. PuddleDancer Press, p. 3. For more information visit www.CNVC.org and www.NonviolentCommunication.com

2 See *Teach Yourself UML in 24 Hours,* by Joseph Schmuller, Sams Publishing, 1999.

3 Interesting video of Jill Bolte Taylor on the brain's hemispheres at http://www.ted.com/talks/jill_bolte_taylor_s_powerful_stroke_of_insight.html

4 Linda Green is commonly attributed as the first person to use this term for "need" in the NVC community.

5 Wikipedia, s.v. "spiritual formation," http://en.wikipedia.org/wiki/Spiritual_formation.

6 See *Sanctification in a New Key: Relieving Evangelical Anxieties over Spiritual Formation* by Steve L. Porter, Journal of Spiritual Formation and Soul Care 2008, Biola University, Vol. 1, No. 2, pp. 129–148.

7 See Matthew 6:24.

8 From Wikipedia, s.v. "major religious groups," http://en.wikipedia.org/wiki/Major_religious_groups.

9 See *The Powers That Be: Theology for a New Millennium,* by Walter Wink. Fortress Press, Minneapolis, MN, p. 31

10 Ibid., pp. 37–97.

11 See *The Secret Message of Jesus: Uncovering the Truth That Could Change Everything* by Brian McLaren. Thomas Nelson, 2006. pp. 129–161.

12 See John 14:15–21.

13 See John 1:14–17.

14 Wikipedia, s.v. "value judgment," http://en.wikipedia.org/wiki/Value_judgment.

15 Wikipedia, s.v. "morality," http://en.wikipedia.org/wiki/Morality.

16 The Tree of Knowledge of Good and Evil is sometimes called the Tree of Knowledge. I resist the temptation to shorten the name of that tree because the shorter name is misleading. God didn't say we couldn't or shouldn't have knowledge; he was concerned with our having specific knowledge: the knowledge of good and evil.

17 It wasn't like *let there be light* and there was light. The text says *commanded,* but it's more of a warning, since he allowed us to choose to eat.

18 See *The Divine Conspiracy: Rediscovering Our Hidden Life in God* by Dallas Willard. HarperCollins, 1997. p. 81.

19 See Romans 2:15

20 See *Resisting the Temptation of Moral Formation: Finding the Spirit in Formation* by Dr. John Coe, Director, Institute for Spiritual Formation, Talbot

School of Theology, 2007. Materials from Rock Harbor Men's Retreat Oct 2007.

[21] See Matthew 22:36–40

[22] See chapters 14.Needs Are Often Confused with Strategies and chapter 35. Motivation: Needs vs. Strategies

[23] I heard this first from Marshall Rosenberg; it originated with Polish-American scientist and philosopher Alfred Korzybski. See http://en.wikipedia.org/wiki/Alfred_Korzybski.

[24] Wikipedia, s.v. "logos," http://en.wikipedia.org/wiki/Logos. See also http://www.pbs.org/faithandreason/theogloss/logos-body.html.

[25] Wikipedia, s.v. "self-similarity," http://en.wikipedia.org/wiki/Self-similarity.

[26] See Mark 12:30–31.

[27] Some of the material in this section was contributed by my friend Garrett Weeks.

[28] The strategy of being a victim can be identified by the use of evaluative words. See chapter 0 for details.

[29] See also *The Powers That Be* by Walter Wink.

[30] *Pagan Christianity* by Frank Viola and George Barna, Present Testimony Ministry, 2003, discusses the effects on the Church of eating from The Tree of Knowledge of Good and Evil.

[31] If you've never tried it, and it's warm outside, I highly recommend running and playing in the rain, provided there's no lightning, it's safe, and your health can handle it.

[32] Wikipedia, s.v. "raggedy andy," http://en.wikipedia.org/wiki/Raggedy_Andy

[33] Wikipedia, s.v. "sin," http://en.wikipedia.org/wiki/Sin.

[34] *Dynamic Catholicism: A Historical Catechism*, by Thomas Bokenkotter. Image Press, 1986. pp. 295–96.

[35] See John 10:10.

[36] See *Things Hidden: Scripture as Spirituality* by Richard Rohr. St. Anthony Messenger Press, 2008, p. 29.

[37] See http://wiki.answers.com/Q/What_is_the_Greek_word_for_%27blessed%27

[38] See http://www.dictionary.net/blessed.

[39] *Jesus and Nonviolence: A Third Way* by Walter Wink, Fortress Press, Minneapolis, pp. 9–16

[40] *Jesus and Nonviolence*, pp. 13, 51.

[41] *The Five Love Languages: How to Express Heartfelt Commitment to Your Mate* by Gary Chapman, Northfield Publishing, 1995.

[42] *The Four Loves* by C. S. Lewis: http://en.wikipedia.org/wiki/The_Four_Loves

43 The New Living Translation (NLT) Bible translates verse 33 as "Then a despised Samaritan came along, and when he saw the man, he felt compassion for him."

44 *The Authentic Gospel of Jesus* by Geza Vermes. London, Penguin Books, 2004. p. 152-154. Emphasis added. Cited at http://en.wikipedia.org/wiki/Parable_of_the_Good_Samaritan.

45 Toys were provided by Try Out Toys Entertainment, www.tryouttoys.com.

46 "Amazing Grace" was played by Tartanic, http://www.tartanic.com/. They played the version with wild and passionate drumming (not the lame drum-set version). See also http://www.youtube.com/watch?v=QOK9yNTdaeQ, http://www.youtube.com/watch?v=ZJSrFnBjjPg.

47 Composed Monday Oct 26, 2009.

48 See Genesis 1:26-31.

49 See also Matthew 18:1-5.

50 Wikipedia, s.v. "self-similarity," see http://en.wikipedia.org/wiki/Self-similarity.

51 See also John 6.

52 This interpretation is consistent with Ephesians 4:29-32 and Acts 4:32-35.

53 From the book Nonviolent Communication by Dr. Marshall B. Rosenberg, pp. 92-93 www.NonviolentCommunication.com

54 Special thanks to my friend Sheri Denham for pointing this out.

55 *The Powers That Be*, pp. 31-36.

56 From notes taken at a session facilitated by Dr. Marshall Rosenberg on Restorative Justice, at an NVC International Intensive Training in December 2007, Albuquerque, New Mexico.

57 *The Powers That Be*, pp. 48-62.

58 See http://haquelebac.wordpress.com/2010/03/29/the-etymology-of-hypocrisy/

59 See *Reimagining Church: Pursuing the Dream of Organic Christianity* by Frank Viola, David C. Cook Publishers, 2008. p. 194.

60 See http://www.katsandogz.com/onjoy.html.

61 See *Things Hidden*, p. 200.

62 *Webster's Online Dictionary*, s.v. "observation," http://www.websters-online-dictionary.org/definition/observation.

63 See also *The Power of Now: A Guide to Spiritual Enlightenment* by Eckhart Tolle, ReadHowYouWant.com, 2010. p. 37.

64 Diagram from Jim & Jori Maske, radicalcompassion.com, Inspired by the work of Marshall Rosenberg, PhD, and Manfred Max-Neef, PhD. Peaceworks, Jim & Jori Manske, www.cnvc.org.

65 Wikipedia, s.v. "Spiritual Exercises of *Ignatius* of Loyola," see http://en.wikipedia.org/wiki/Spiritual_Exercises_of_Ignatius_of_Loyola

[66] See http://ignatianspirituality.com/making-good-decisions/an-approach-to-good-choices/ and http://norprov.org/spirituality/ignatianprayer.htm

[67] *Dynamic Catholicism*, p. 307.

[68] Mary Mackenzie, Flagstaff Center for Compassionate Communication, www.compassionatecommunication.org

[69] Marshall Rosenberg, The Center for Nonviolent Communication. www.cnvc.org.

[70] Based on work by Robert Gonzales, Robert@living-compassion.org.

[71] *Sadhana: A Way to God: Christian Exercises in Eastern Form* by Anthony de Mello, Image Books, 1984. See also *The Song of the Bird* by Anthony de Mello, Image Books, 1982.

[72] Empathy, a workshop by Robert Gonzales, December 2007 at International Intensive Training in Albuquerque NM. See The Prescott Center for Nonviolent Communication, http://www.prescottnvc.org/.

[73] Jim and Jori Manske, http://www.radicalcompassion.org/. "As far as I know we were the first to use in the NVC Community, but of course with 200+ trainers and rare published works (other than handouts), it's hard to know for sure. It is an adaptation of a well-known NLP technique called Meta-Outcoming that I first learned from my NLP trainer, Robert Dilts, in 1991." For more on Meta-Outcoming, see http://nlpuniversitypress.com/html2/MdMe17.html.

[74] For contact information, go to www.CompassionateConnecting.com

[75] Translation by Clive Scott based on Erasmus's translation of *logos* as *conversation*. I thank Dan Tocchini of ACCD for inspiring me with Prof. Scott's work during my Breakthrough training.

Made in the USA
Lexington, KY
19 October 2011